YOU DON'T KNOW G. A. C.
(GEORGE ARMSTRONG CUSTER)

Quizzes and Trivia from
Custer Battlefield Historical
& Museum Association

Authors
Dennis Farioli
Vincent Heier
Tom Pream

Editor
Nora L. Whitley

Custer Battlefield Historical & Museum Association, Inc.

ISBN 1-892258-04-8

Published in 1999
Copy editing, layout & design by Old Army Press
Printed by Citizen Printing Company
Fort Collins, Colorado

Custer Battlefield Historical & Museum Association, Inc.
P.O. Box 902
Hardin, Montana   59034-0902

TABLE OF CONTENTS

(Continued on page 4)

LIST OF ILLUSTRATIONS

PREFACE

And let the spot where Custer fell
Be marked by shaft enduring, high,
That to all ages e're shall tell
The story that can never die.

A.P. Kerr

Twenty years ago, Neil C. Mangum, serving as the historian for the Custer Battlefield National Monument, penned the first set of quiz questions for the Custer Battlefield Historical and Museum Association. This quiz consisted of only ten questions, but became the foundation for all future quizzes. Tom Pream has assembled a complete set of the CBHMA. annual quizzes and their answers. Tom has also carefully noted the author and winner of each quiz. In addition to collecting twenty years of CBHMA quizzes, Tom titled our book, *You Don't Know G.A.C.*

Ron Nichols, Mardell Plain Feather and Chris Summitt compiled a set of ten questions for the third annual CBHMA quiz. Since then, the annual CBHMA. quiz has had such distinguished authors as: Tim Bernardis, Doug McChristian, Tom Pream, Vincent Heier and Dennis Farioli. Currently the annual quiz is twenty questions in length and is a challenge to answer all questions correctly. Authors of the annual quiz have researched hundreds of Custer related books to come up with their difficult and obscure questions. This research has lead to an amazing collection of trivia, little-known and obscure facts about the Plains Indian Wars, Custer, the Battle of Little Big Horn, the Little Bighorn Battlefield National Monument and all those men who fought as scouts, soldiers or civilians in this well remembered battle.

Who has won the greatest number of CBHMA. annual quizzes? Gary Gilbert and Dale Kosman share that distinction (at this writing), each winning three. Who was the winner of Quiz Number 1? James E. Reach of Covington, Ohio won the first quiz in 1980. When called upon to find a missing piece of this book, Quiz Number 2 and its answers, Dale Kosman had it in his collection. In addition, Dale supplied me with a list of the authors of the annual quizzes.

Tom Pream, a collector and historian, found an unpublished photo of Autie Reed which is included in this book. Not only has Mr. Pream written the first section of *You Don't Know G.A.C.*, he has written quizzes and has submitted the winning answers to the annual quiz (when he was not the author). His fellow authors thank Tom for all of his hours of work on *You Don't Know G. A. C.*

The annual quizzes comprise the first section of this collection. The second section is the first-hand account of Alfred Chapman, an individual who claims he witnessed the Battle of Little Big Horn and lived to tell a reporter from the *San Francisco Examiner* about his adventure. What a tall tale! After the wildly imaginative report of Alfred Chapman, *You Don't Know G.A.C.* continues with a section compiled by Dennis Farioli of trivia questions and facts. Dennis conceived the idea of this book. He began writing in March of 1997 and has continued to work closely with me throughout its production. Laced throughout Dennis' section is a collection of rarely seen, unpublished or newly-found photos relating to those who were scouts, U.S. Army enlisted men or civilians who fought and died in the Battle of Little Big Horn. The most significant of those to Dennis is the unpublished photo of Captain William McCaskey which is included in our collection and used with the permission of Hank Chapman, great grandson of Captain McCaskey. Dennis is currently collecting materials for a new book on Captain McCaskey, who was the commander of Fort Abraham Lincoln in Custer's absence. In addition, as a living historian and historical re-enactor, Mr. Farioli portrays Captain McCaskey. Near and dear to my heart is the never before published photo of young Autie Reed and his two friends found in this section of the book. This photo was found by our fellow author, Tom Pream. I portray Mrs. David Reed, mother of Autie Reed, in my capacity as a living historian re-enactor and this heretofore unpublished photo of Autie Reed is a welcome addition to our book. Many thanks to Dennis, his wife, Rosemary and daughter, Teressa, for all of their collected hard work with this project.

Vincent Heier has outdone himself with his collection of trivia on the subjects of novels, art, movie and TV which comprise the next section of this book. Never before have I read such facts! Read and learn the answers to such questions as: In the romance novel, *Cody's*

Last Stand, what is the unique connection between lovers Cody and Elizabeth? You are just going to have to read this book to find the answer. We wish to acknowledge the submission of Vince's collection of movie stills depicting all those who have portrayed General Custer in the movies. Due to lack of production time, these photos cannot be published in this book, but we look forward to Vince publishing this exciting collection in the future.

The authors and I wish to thank the following people: Dee and Mike Koury of Old Army Press in Fort Collins, Colorado, for all of their help and advice and their speedy production of this book; Joyce and Ron Nichols, of Broken Arrow Books, for always lending a helping hand and the benefit of their experience; Jahnis Abelite for his computer expertise and Dave Evans and Earl Hunsicker for proof reading..

My fellow authors, Dennis Farioli, Vince Heier, Tom Pream and I are proud to present, *You Don't Know G. A. C.* (pronounced "Jack," the nickname Custer's men gave him based upon his initials) to the Custer Battlefield Historical and Museum Association as a fund raising project. As a special note, each one of us has donated our time and talent to produce and write this book to aid the research, education and fund raising projects CBHMA supports.

Nora L. Whitley
Seattle, Washington

INTRODUCTION
THE BATTLE OF THE
LITTLE BIG HORN

By Nora L. Whitley

There is as much unknown as there is known about what happened June 25, 1876 to Custer and his men. Some say everyone was killed, no survivors. Others say, of course there were survivors, the Indians. Then, there are the first-hand accounts of "survivors" such as Alfred L. Chapman, who was at the Battle of Little Big Horn only in his imagination. From the moment Custer gave his last order to Reno and began heading north, the events that followed are not truly known. The only real certainty is the U. S. Army suffered one of the worse defeats recorded during the Plains Indian Wars. From the time of the defeat of the military at the Little Big Horn, a steady decline of the living conditions of the Native Americans in the United States began.

Much controversy is attached to this battle. Even the actual numbers of men killed and wounded is reported differently among historians. I will stand by the count of 268 killed and 60 wounded of those counted in the U. S. Army. Such a count of killed and wounded among the warriors is impossible for me to state. Historians also differ in opinion on how many warriors participated in the Battle of the Little Big Horn. One point agreed upon is the U. S. Army was outnumbered that day.

The news of Custer's demise hit the newspapers and telegraphs just as our nation was celebrating its centennial in 1876 thus launching this nation into its second century with the sad shadow of loss on its celebrations.

Alfred Chapman
San Francisco Examiner - approximately 1907

A.L. Chapman, one of the last of the old scouts.

A. L. Chapman Saw the 7th Cavalry Slaughtered by Sioux Indians

One white man who witnessed the Custer massacre still survives, according to the narrative of Alfred Chapman, who was a scout under General George Armstrong Custer in the latter's Indian campaign between 1873 and the spring of 1876, and who resides at 1024 Franklin Street, San Francisco. Chapman says he saw the fight from the opening skirmish until Custer himself, the last to fall, was slain.

Chapman is a native of California, having been born at Marysville, March 4, 1849. He speaks seven Indian languages, and says he served Custer as scout and guide for three years.

"Mrs. Custer mentions me twice in her book, *Boots and Saddles*," Chapman says. "She calls me the 'citizen guide.'"

Several weeks before the Custer battle Chapman says he was captured by the Indians and held a prisoner for eighteen days on the Little Missouri, in Dakota Territory. He contrived to escape and was following Custer, endeavoring to rejoin his command, when he came upon the memorable battle on the Little Big Horn.

INDIANS CAPTURE HIM

"I left Fort Abraham Lincoln with Custer and Terry in April, 1876," Chapman says. "Fort Lincoln was only a few miles from Bismarck. We scouts were kept in the advance continuously, for we were moving through hostile country, and I was headed off by some Sioux Indians under old Chief Tin Cup and made a prisoner on the Little Missouri River on May 30, 1876.

"The Indians took my horse, and when I escaped, at midnight on June 17th, I started back for Fort Lincoln on foot. I reached the fort June 19th, got another horse and rations for a week and started out on the trail the command had taken. I could not follow the trail too closely, for the country was full of Indians. I had to mark the trail and travel by night or through the broken country off to one side of it, under cover as much as possible. I saw Indians every day, but I did not see any large bands of them until I got close to Custer.

"I was skirting the heads of the draws in the bluffs on the easterly side of the Little Big Horn on the morning of June 25th, when I discovered Custer's command down in the valley. The troops were about three miles away, and the formation told me they were not Indians, although their movements made me think there was business on hand.

HORSE IS CONCEALED

"I left my horse in a coulee - you call it an arroyo in California - and crawled up to the edge of the bluffs, where I studied the situation through my glasses. I was too far away to see well, so I went back, got my horse and rode further up the ridge, keeping out of sight. I left my horse again and moved on my stomach as far out on the bluffs as I could with safety. I could see a few Indians dashing across the valley on their horses. The ground between me and Custer appeared open, and I thought I could make it, but before trying I dropped my glass over it. Several time I swept it without seeing anything unusual.

"I could identify Custer and other officials plainly from where I lay. The command had halted for a few minutes and I could see Custer swinging one arm. Then Reno and Benteen and their men pulled off to one side, and Custer started straight ahead, coming almost in my direction. I threw my glasses across the ground ahead of him, and saw the head of an Indian peering

above the sagebrush at the approaching troops. That made me search the sagebrush more closely, and I could see their moccasins, too. There were lying behind the sagebrush, and it seemed to me that there was an Indian for every sagebrush over a quarter section of the land.

FURIOUS BATTLE BEGFNS

"Then the firing began. At first there were only scattering shots, as the Indians in front discharged their guns and began failing back. I saw Reno and Benteen as they started over the ridge, and saw them beaten back. I saw Custer coming swinging up the side hill at the head of his men, following a handful of Indians, and I saw the Indians I had been counting in the sagebrush spring out from their hiding places and sweep in behind and before him. The firing became furious then and the smoke was heavy. I knew he had been trapped, for I could see that the inequalities of the ground had made it impossible for him to see the Indians. Then I saw Indians pouring in from behind a hill — Indians that I had not been able to see before — and I realized then that the trap was worse than it had appeared even to me.

"Still I knew Custer for the greatest Indian fighter that ever lived, and I thought he would pull through. I was sure he would if only Reno or Benteen could reach him. For a few minutes the black powder smoke was so thick I could not tell just how the thing was going with Custer, so I watched Reno and Benteen. I saw they were hemmed in, and I thought the Indians were wiping them out.

SHELLS STICK IN GUNS

"I turned my glasses back to Custer. By that time the firing was not so heavy, and I could see more clearly. The old boys of the Seventh were completely corralled. The Indians were circling them but keeping at a respectful distance. The soldiers were returning their fire, but I could see that they were not reloading as rapidly as they should. I knew what the trouble was, for I had experienced the results where verdigris attacked my cartridge shells so the base of a shell would pull off and leave the case stuck in the chamber of the gun.

"I could see hundreds of soldiers sprawled on the ground, dead and dying, but still Custer stood firing, first with a rifle, then with revolvers. The Indians were crowding in more closely by that time, and I could see them clubbing soldiers to death as they ran in and dashed out again.

"Custer was the last man on his feet. There was no smoke to interfere with my vision by that time, for there was scarcely any firing. I could make out just how Custer was dressed — top boots to his knees, buckskin trousers fringed on the sides, a dark blue flannel shirt and a broad- brimmed hat. He was waving a six-shooter about his head. A dozen Indians were rushing at him firing as they ran. I turned my eyes — I did not want to see him fall. When I looked again he was not to be seen.

BUTCHERY BEGINS

"Indians were dashing about the battlefield by the thousand, scalping and mutilating the soldiers. Custer's body was the only one that was not molested. I decided not to move until I saw what direction the Indians took. For a time everything was quiet over where Benteen and Reno lay, and I felt sure they, too. had been slaughtered. Then there came a fusillade, and I knew they were still holding out.

"In a short time I saw all the Indians leave the Custer field and move off up the river to the south. Some accounts say they went north, but I know better, for I was there and saw them — loading their wounded and dead on travois and striking out rapidly, leaving only enough to hold Reno and Benteen.

"I made my way back to my horse and slept out in the bluffs that night. My rations had been consumed, and I ate rosebuds. The next day I located and joined Terry's command. I knew it was impossible for me to get through to Reno and Benteen, and then I fully expected they would be cleaned up before the Indians left them.

"Curly, a full-blooded Crow scout, always said he had been with Custer until the fighting got hot, then threw a blanket over his head and got away. Curly would never meet me, for he had shown cowardice and when he learned that I had seen the fight he knew I was aware of his treachery. Curly really left an hour or more before the fight began. And he did not follow orders. Custer had told him to find Terry and tell him he was going to attack the Indians. Curly should have gone north, but instead of that he took the opposite direction and kept going."

This original San Francisco Examiner *article was provided by Hank Chapman, great-grandson of Capt. William S. McCaskey and no relation to Alfred Chapman.*

CBHMA ANNUAL QUIZ 1980-1999

By Tom Pream

The following section of this book represents the entire collection of CBHMA annual quizzes with the names of the authors and quiz winners for each year. There are twenty quizzes in all with different authors for each quiz. Beginning with Quiz 1, written by Neil Mangum in 1980, the annual CBHMA Quiz boasts a roster of familiar and well known authors within the organization.

Each year, CBHMA publishes its annual quiz in *The Battlefield Dispatch's* spring issue. The answers are printed in the following summer issue. Over the years, the quiz has grown from ten questions to twenty questions in length. Readers will notice in some years the quiz is only eight questions in length. In 1995 and 1996, there were fifteen questions in the annual quiz. The number of questions are determined by the quiz author. In 1994 a tie-breaker question was offered.

Since this is a trivia book, I will include a few more statistics about the annual CBHMA quizzes, its authors and winners. Neil Mangum has authored five of the twenty quizzes. Doug McChristian is the author of four quizzes. Chris Summitt and Ron Nichols each authored two quizzes. Ron Nichols is on record as winning the quiz in 1981 — no, he was not the author of it. The team of Vincent Heier and Dennis Farioli has authored five quizzes. I won the annual quiz in 1989 and authored 1993's Quiz 14.

Who is our youngest winner? Teressa Farioli, who was two at the time, shared a win of Quiz 13 with Gary Gilbert in 1992. She is a born and bred Custer buff and a lifetime member of CBHMA. Our kepi's off to Teressa for this remarkable accomplishment. Her father, Dennis, won in 1986 and 1988.

Which individual has been the most frequent winner of the annual quiz? Gary Gilbert and Dale Kosman tie for this honor. I will add that one of Gary's wins was accomplished in a coin toss between he and Dale.

I encourage you to read and study this collection of quizzes. They are a valuable tool for any student of this remarkable period.

1980 – QUIZ NUMBER 1

Winner – James E. Rench of Covington, Ohio

Author - Neil Mangum

1. Who was the 7th Cavalry officer who is quoted as saying, "A good soldier has to serve two mistresses. While he's loyal to one the other must suffer"?

2. Name George Custer's two dogs who remained behind with the pack train during the battle of the Little Big Horn?

3. Prior to the Battle of the Little Big Horn, the Sioux and Cheyenne camp was joined by a band of Arapahoes. They were considered spies and believed to have aided Crook in the Rosebud fight. One leading chief intervened on their behalf and probably saved their lives. Name this Indian.

4. Which two officers rode out to meet the advance elements of Terry's and Gibbon's troops marching up the Little Big Horn?

5. In September, 1875, a special commission assembled near Red Cloud Agency in an attempt to purchase the Black Hills from the Indians. Name the leader of this commission.

6. After Custer's death, who replaced him as lieutenant colonel of the 7th Cavalry?

7. Lt. Frank Gibson returned to Fort Abraham Lincoln where he married the sister of Lt. Donald McIntosh's wife. Who was the bride and best man at the wedding?

8. Which three officers present at the battle celebrate their birthdays on the same day?

9. Name two messengers sent by Reno to Custer after Reno found Indians to his front.

10. Name the son of Sitting Bull who was killed with his father at Standing Rock Agency, December 15, 1890.

Answers to the annual quizzes start on page 41

1981 – QUIZ NUMBER 2

Winner – Ron Nichols, California

Author – Neil Mangum

1. General Custer was born on December 5, 1839, as anyone who knows anything about the subject will readily agree. What well known Indian, who fought Custer at the Little Big Horn, died on Custer's birthday in 1894?

2. Who made the buckskin suit Custer was wearing on his last campaign?

3. When General Terry was ascending the valley of the Little Big Horn on June 26, 1876, he offered a $200 bonus to two of his scouts if they would deliver a dispatch to Custer. Name the two scouts who accepted the offer, but could not get through.

4. Name the brother-in-law of George Yates who accompanied the 1876 expedition.

5. Name the three Arikara scouts killed in Reno's valley fight.

6. With which band of Sioux was Hump affiliated?

7. Which company was pulled out of Reno's skirmish line to support the horse holders in the timber during the valley fight?

8. What 7th Cavalry officer is quoted as saying, "Gentlemen, in my opinion, General Custer has made the biggest mistake of his life by not taking the whole regiment in at once in the first attack."?

9. "The Forty Thieves" is a sobriquet applied to what company of the 7th Cavalry in the 1870's?

10. Who was the Crow interpreter who signed on with Gibbon but was left on the Yellowstone after sustaining a broken collar bone in a fall from his horse and missed the final stage of the Little Big Horn campaign?

Answers to the annual quizzes start on page 41

1982 – QUIZ NUMBER 3

Winner - Mrs. Geraldine Toupin of Gore's Landing, Ontario, Canada

Authors - Ron Nichols, Mardell Plain Feather and Chris Summitt

I. During the 1876 campaign, for supply purposes, the columns from Lincoln and Montana relied on two steamboats- *The Far West* and _____ ?

2. Who said "Custer is happy now, off with a roving command for fifteen days"?

3. During Reno's initial charge against the Indians in the valley, several private soldiers completely lost control of their horses, which ran away with them and into and through the swirling bands of Indians. Name three of these troopers.

4. Who made the statement, "We had no protection . . . we were being surrounded . . . I think Reno did the only thing possible under the circumstances. If we had remained in the timber all would have been killed"? Which of the 7th Cavalry officers killed at the Little Big Horn was reburied in Auburn, New York on October 25, 1877?

6. Mary Hannah Ross in 1863 married a military man who was to become an officer in the 7th Cavalry and would participate in the Battle of the Little Big Horn. Who was he?

7. Which 7th Cavalry officer participated in the campaign against the Nez Perce and was severely wounded at the Battle of Snake Creek in the Bear Paw Mountains?

8. How old was Sitting Bull at the time of the Battle of the Little Big Horn?

9. Which of the six Crow scouts was wounded?

10. During Custer's engagement in the Battle of the Little Big Horn, a warrior named Lame White Man was killed. He was visiting the Indian encampment at the time of the battle. To what tribe did he belong?

Answers to the annual quizzes start on page 41

1983 - QUIZ NUMBER 4

Winner - Bobby Reece of Longmont, Colorado

Author - Chris Summitt

Quotes From the Little Big Horn

Name the persons who made the following statements:

1. "Oh my God, I have got it."

2. "What is this, a retreat? It looks damnably like a rout "

3. "What damn fool move is this?"

4. "There go your Indians running like devils."

5. "For God's sake boys, don't run. Don't let them whip us "

6. "I have a very sad report to make. I have counted 197 bodies lying in the hills."

7. "All around the Indians began jumping up and running forward, dodging down, jumping up again, all the time going toward the soldiers."

8. "We've had a big fight in the valley and got whipped like hell."

9. "We shoot, we ride fast, we shoot again."

10. "Know the power that is peace."

Answers to the annual quizzes start on page 41

1984 - QUIZ NUMBER 5

Winner – William R. O'Donnel of Cheyenne, Wyoming

Author - Tim Bernardis

Quotes From the Little Big Horn

Name the persons who made the following statements:

1. "It seemed that peace and happiness were prevailing all over the world. That nowhere was any man planning to lift his hand against his fellow man.''

2. "Because of the dust, it was impossible to see any distance and the rattle of equipment and clattering of the horses' feet made it difficult to hear distinctly beyond your immediate surroundings."

3. "That plan is bad! It should not be carried out."

4. "Who in the mischief moved that command?"

5. "From the divide could be seen the valley of the Little Big Horn, and about 15 to 20 miles to the northwest could be seen a light blue cloud, and to the practiced eye showed that our game was near."

6. "It'd be easy to say we were thinking only of glory on this hot June Sunday afternoon, but I reckon what most of the plain troopers were thinking about was how good a nice cold bottle of beer would taste. We knew this was the day."

7. "But if we go in there, we will never come out alive."

8. "Here was the 7th Cavalry, with a total of 600 men, split into four outfits, Indian hunting in a rolling, mountainous country, far removed from civilization."

9. "I had been a good deal in Indian country and was convinced that they were there in overwhelming numbers."

10. ". . . if the soldiers had not fired until all of them were ready for the attack, if they had brought their horses and rode into the camp of the Sioux, the power of the Dakota Nation might have been broken and our young men killed in the surprise . . ."

Answers to the annual quizzes start on page 41

1985 - QUIZ NUMBER 6

Winner – John Husk of Englewood, Colorado.

Author - credit is given to Neil Mangum

1. What was the title of the first movie ever produced about the battle of Little Big Horn?

2. Custer was not the youngest general of the U.S. Army to wear the star of a brigadier general. Name one who was younger.

3. In what year was the iron fence erected around the "Last Stand" group of 52 stones?

4. Name the two officers who fought at the Little Big Horn who are now interred in the Custer Battlefield National Cemetery?

5. Iron Hail, a young Minneconjou warrior who fought here, and later at Wounded Knee, is also known by what other name?

6. Who said, "If we had remained in the river bottom twenty minutes longer, not a man of us would have escaped"?

7. Pretty Shield was the wife of which Crow scout?

8. Which officer positively identified surgeon Edwin Lord's remains as being in the "Last Stand" group?

9. Which of Custer's Crow scouts lived the longest, passing away on June 2, 1929?

10. Which 7th Cavalry officer attended the U.S. Naval Academy for two years?

Answers to the annual quizzes start on page 41

1986 - QUIZ NUMBER 7

Winner - Dennis Farioli of Hampden, Massachusetts

Author - Neil Mangum

1. What is the name of Crazy Horse's wife?

2. What army officer said this about Sitting Bull: "The great organizer and controlling spirit of the hostile element. None of the other Indians possesed the power of drawing and molding the hearts of his people to one purpose''?

3. In what year did William White begin guide service at Custer Battlefield? White was with Gibbon's command which discovered the bodies of Custer's men June 27, 1876.

4. Which of Custer's scouts wrote a book titled *E-Sack-Wattee Stories*, which used a coyote to recount the tales?

5. Which of the Seventh Cavalry officers killed at Little Big Horn are buried at Fort Leavenworth?

6. Who said this about Custer's defeat, "It was an unnecessary sacrifice due to misapprehension and superabundant courage, the latter extraordinarily developed in Custer"?

7. Give the date of the dedication of the Custer Battlefield Visitor Center and Museum.

8. Who is the author of *The Last Battle of the Sioux Nation?*

9. In the opinion of George Custer, which West Point class was the finest for producing officers?

10. Upon receiving Custer's message "to come on . . ." to which officer did Benteen first show the message?

Answers to the annual quizzes start on page 41

1987 - QUIZ NUMBER 8

Winner – Trudy Forbes of Seattle, Washington

Author - credit is given to Neil Mangum

1. This man was Reno's orderly. During the retreat from the woods, his horse went down but he recovered and made it to the safety of the bluffs. Name this soldier.

2. What noted Indian warrior claimed that all of Custer's men were dead by the time soldiers reached Weir Point?

3. Name the Montana column officer who began mapping the Custer Battlefield but was stopped by Lt. Maquire who claimed that the mapping should be completed under his supervision?

4. Name the warrior who scalped one side of Lt. William W. Cooke's elongated beard?

5. According to Pretty Shield, where did Custer die?

6. In what year did Two Moon, Cheyenne warrior, die?

7. Name the seven civilians killed in the battle of the Little Big Horn.

8. Who was known by the Crows as "Two Bodies?"

9. In what year did the War Department transfer Lt. John J. Crittenden's remains from the battlefield to the national cemetery?

10. In 1925 a delegation of Cheyennes headed by Mrs. Thomas Beaverheart petitioned the battlefield to erect a marker for a Cheyenne killed in the fight. The request was denied. Name the Cheyenne for whom the marker was intended.

Answers to the annual quizzes start on page 41

1988 – QUIZ NUMBER 9

Winner - Dennis Farioli of Hampden, Massachusetts

Author – no information regarding the author is available

Who Am I?

1. I was befriended by Captain Miles Keogh. My death, occurring November 6, 1891, was less tragic than his.

2. I was honored with a monument on September 17, 1938, showing where I fell in the Battle of the Little Big Horn.

3. I was with the Gibbon - Terry column serving in the capacity of surgeon.

4. I met General Godfrey on Custer Ridge June 25, 1926. I shook his hand and presented him with my blanket. He reciprocated by giving me an American flag.

5. Muggins Taylor reached my ranch on the Stillwater River and told me of the Custer disaster. I proffered Taylor a fresh mount and rode with him the next morning to Bozeman. I took the message of Custer's demise to Helena.

6. I was embroiled romantically with my "Bachelor Boy" (Custer) in 1856.

7. During Custer's last battle I heard Lame White Man call: "Young men come now with me and show yourselves to be brave."

8. I was superintendent of the Custer Battlefield when it changed its name from Custer Battlefield National Cemetery to Custer Battlefield National Monument.

9. I was a noted warrior at the Little Big Horn, I died October 14, 1905.

10. I am the artist of the drawing "Indians Leaving Battle Ground."

Answers to the annual quizzes start on page 41

1989 - QUIZ NUMBER 10

Winner – Tom Pream of Arden Hills, Minnesota.

Author – no information is available regarding the author

1. Name the soldier who was killed on the withdrawal from Weir Point.

2. Of the soldiers of the 7th Cavalry who were killed in the battle June 25 - 26, 1876, how many are buried in the Custer Battlefield National Cemetery?

3. During the Civil War, Custer captured a sword from a Confederate officer. What is the original inscription on the blade?

4. Two forts in the West were named "Reno." Where were they located and which one was named after Major Marcus A. Reno?

5. One thing Lt. Charles Varnum could not train his personal mare to do was _____?

6. In what ways did General Montgomery Meigs permanently influence Custer Battlefield?

7. Who commanded the 1881 reburial detail on Custer Battlefield?

8. There was a Custer in Company I, 7th Cavalry, during the Indian Wars. Who was he and when did he serve?

9. The man who signed Reno's exoneration papers is a relative of which significant person in Reno's military career?

10. Name the four designated sharpshooters covering the water carriers on June 26.

Answers to the annual quizzes start on page 41

1990 - QUIZ NUMBER 11

Winners - Joy and Gary Gilbert of Cape Girardeau, Missouri

Author - Doug McChristian

1. If you called *8459 Lenox* in May of 1912, who would answer the phone?

2. Up to 1876, which 7th Cavalry officer had been given the highest number of demerits at West Point?

3. Who were the Medal of Honor winners at the Little Big Horn who were not water carriers or sharpshooters? (Hint: There were five.)

4. Who conducted the funeral for Custer at West Point?

5. What role did the following men share: Capt. Wm. McCaskey, Lt. C.L. Gurley and Dr. J.V.D. Middleton?

6. Name the Cheyenne warrior who was given the honorary distinction of having killed Custer?

7. A 7th Cavalry horse was mounted by Prof. Dyche and exhibited at the World's Fair in Chicago and St. Louis. Whose horse was it? (Hint: it was NOT COMANCHE.)

8. How much pension money did Libby receive each month after 12 years as an officer's wife?

9. In 1932, Lt. Crittenden's stone and remains were moved from Calhoun Hill to the national cemetery. In what year was a marble marker placed for him on the battlefield?

10. Who was the last person to ride Dandy, Custer's favorite horse?

Answers to the annual quizzes start on page 41

1991 QUIZ NUMBER 12

Winner - Bryan Curtis of Aurora, Colorado

Author - Doug McChristian

1. Who was responsible for George Custer's first permanent physical scar?

2. Name the enlisted men in the Battle of the Little Big Horn who were half-brothers.

3. Who said, "I did not think it possible that any white men would attack us, so strong as we were"?

4. Name the only 7th Cavalryman in the Battle of the Little Big Horn to have served previously as a U.S. Marine.

5. Who was the last surviving officer of the Battle of the Little Big Horn? Bonus point if you know the date of his death.

6. What was the name of Capt. Myles W. Keogh's second mount, which was left with the pack train? Hint: The horse was government and survived the battle.

7. Name the warrior who tried to count coup on Pvt. James J. Tanner of Company M. Bonus point if you know the tribe.

8. Which 7th Cavalry surgeon had an MD from Harvard Medical School and flunked the Army Medical Board exam?

9. What did Capt. Thomas W. Custer and Pvt. William Brown have in common that no other 7th Cavalry man can claim?

10. Name the youngest and oldest soldier killed with Custer: Bonus if you know their age at death.

Answers to the annual quizzes start on page 41

1992 QUIZ NUMBER 13

Winners - Gary Gilbert of Cape Girardeau, Missouri
and
Teressa Farioli of Hampden, Massachusetts

Author - Doug McChristian

1. Name the two 7th Cavalrymen who fired the last shots at the Battle of the Little Big Horn. Hint one was an officer and the other a noncommissioned officer.

2. Name three of the songs sung by some of the officers at the June 24, 1876 evening bivouac near modern day Busby, Montana.

3. Who was the Sioux warrior who was shot down in front of White Bull during the Reno hilltop fight?

4. The Reno Benteen Battlefield was first known as_____.

5. When was the present memorial erected at the Reno Benteen Battlefield?

6. How many 7th Cavalry soldiers died of wounds aboard the riverboat *Far West* on the journey to Fort Abraham Lincoln? Bonus point if you can name the men and the dates of death.

7. What was the name of the Cheyenne warrior who captured an army bugle during the battle, tried to make a call and, with practice, latter succeeded?

8. When was the present low iron fence erected on Last Stand Hill?

9. Who said, "Men this is a groundhog case; it is live or die with us. We must fight it out with them"? Bonus point if you can give the exact date it was said.

10. Lt. Col. George A. Custer was one of three army officers killed in action at or above the rank of lieutenant colonel. Name the other two. Hint: they were killed after 1866.

Answers to the annual quizzes start on page 41

1993 QUIZ NUMBER 14
Winner - Wayne M. Sarf of Riverdale New Jersey
Authors - Tom Pream and Vince Heier

1. This F Troop private claimed to have been with Custer's command at Ford B when his horse bolted and carried him unharmed through the Hunkpapa camp and up onto Reno Hill at 4:00 P.M.

2. The English translation of the name Custer is the occupation of _____.

3. Match the names of the participants of the 1876 campaign in the left column with their not so well known names on the right by printing the letter next to that name in the corresponding blank.

0. **Doug McChristian**	_K_	A	Kapesh
1. Charlie Reynolds	____	B	Man with dark face
2. Fred Gerard	____	C	Chief with a red nose
3. Capt. Thomas French	____	D	Seven Yanktons
4. Col. John Gibbon	____	E	Lucky Man
5. Maj. Marcus A. Reno	____	F	Tucker
6. Lt. George Wallace	____	G	Nes I Ri Pat
7. Bloody Knife	____	H	Crazy Horse
8. Lt. Col. G.A. Custer	____	I -	Nick
9. Mitch Bouyer	____	J	Ouches
10.Charles Varnum	____	K	**Alex Trebek with funny hat**

4. Joe Bush of I Company 7th U.S. Cavalry was seen on the field the day after the Battle of the Little Big Horn. Why doesn't his name appear on any of the company rosters?

5. Lt. C.C. DeRudio was involved in a plot to assassinate _____.

6. On February 3, 1877 the territorial legislature of Montana resolved to do this to the Little Big Horn River?

7. The character actor (a)_____ played Sitting Bull in the motion picture (b) _____ and also played Gen. Phil Sheridan in a movie entitled (c) _____.

8. Custer's striker John Burkeman's most prized possessions were two twenty dollar gold pieces. In what significant years were these coins minted?

9. Which 7th Cavalry officer was dismissed from the army in 1863 for being in Washington without permission and then re-enlisted under the alias of Charles Thomas?

10. The first memorial to G.A. Custer was built at _____, in the year ____; the second memorial was built in _____, in the year ____.

Answers to the annual quizzes start on page 41

1994 - QUIZ NUMBER 15

Winner - Vicky Atchison Peck of Butte, Montana

Author - Tom Pream

1. During Reno's charge to the bluffs, a private from F Company engaged in a hand-to-hand fight with an Indian. In the course of the fight, his horse was killed and the trooper shot the Indian, captured his pony and rejoined the fleeing command. Name this capable trooper.

2. When the original marble markers were sent to the battlefield, none were sent for the civilians who had been killed. Who supplied the marker for Mark Kellogg?

3. Name the war chief whose brother's body was discovered in the "Lone Tepee."

4. Private _____ of H Company accidentally shot himself in the calf while mounting his horse on June 6, 1876 and missed the battle.

5. During the retreat from the valley fight Private _____ was killed with Dr. DeWolf, after nearly reaching the crest of a bluff topped with Indians.

6. Everyone knows that a private in the regular army was paid $13.00 a month for his first two years, but what was a private's pay after two years?

7. Private Edward Dellienhousen was killed at the Little Big Horn but his name is not on the monument. Who was this private and what name is on the monument?

8. Who was Ba-tsida-crush?

9. Who, when asked at the Reno Court of Inquiry, "Wouldn't you sooner have been dejected on top of the hill than dead in the timber?" replied, "I would rather be dejected on top of the hill than dead anywhere."

10. Tie breaker question: What was the correct number of demerits Cadet Marcus A. Reno collected while at West Point? (answers over 1000 are incorrect)

Answers to the annual quizzes start on page 41

1995 - QUIZ NUMBER 16

Winner - Dale Kosman of Lombard, Illinois

Authors - Dennis Farioli and Vincent Heier

1. Marcus A. Reno was injured while leading a charge against Fitzhugh Lee, near Rappahannock during the Civil War. What was the nature of his injury?

2. This man came at Major Reno with a knife, after Reno threatened to shoot him while on route to the Little Big Horn. Who was he?

3. It was reported that this red-headed 7th Cavalryman lost his head June 25, 1876. Who was he?

4. A memorial plaque hangs in the Scottish Church in Edinburgh for this 7th Cavalry member, killed in the Battle of the Little Big Horn, for he was of noble birth. Who was he?

5. _____was at Gettysburg and was General Buford's favorite aide.

6. A Sioux chief, Red Bead, was found dead with an officer. Who was the officer?

7. The actor friend of G.A. Custer, Lawrence Barrett, was born on _____ and died on _____.

8. In 1874, 150 well-armed civilians from Bozeman, Montana, killed scores of Indians along the same route the 7th Cavalry would travel two years later. One of those men rode with Custer to the Little Big Horn. Who was he?

9. Crazy Horse had a younger brother called _____.

10. Edward, Augustus, Sophia and Harriet were the brothers and sisters of whom?

11. "This wild man" and "the insufferable ass" were references to Custer made by what officer?

12. _____, a retired regular soldier, became the first superintendent of the Custer Battlefield National Cemetery on what date?

13. Which one of Custer's scouts gained experience and training under Jim Bridger?

14. On August 11, 1873, _____, using Custer's own Springfield, dropped three warriors in a row, before being shot through the brain.

Answers to the annual quizzes start on page 41

15. Of this company commander in the 7th Cavalry, Alfred Barnitz said that "____ was very slovenly and lazy and unmilitary and I would not give one good non-commissioned officer for half a dozen lieutenants like him."

1996 - QUIZ NUMBER 17

Winner - Dale Kosman of Lombard, Illinois

Authors - Dennis Farioli and Vincent Heier

1. On what date, after the Battle of the Little Big Horn, did the 7th Cavalry return to Ft. Lincoln and under whose command?

2. While Captain Benteen was away, testifying at the Reno Court of Inquiry, what were his quarters being used for?

3. ____ carried the mail for Fort Stevenson and other Missouri River forts overland from Fort Totten, prior to his death June 25, 1876.

4. With Custer's immediate command on June 25, 1876 ____ was killed by Sioux Indians, but not in 1876.

5. On June 10, 1876, Major Reno, with six companies, left on a scout. Who was in charge of the Gatling detatchment on this scout?

6. Who placed wooden stakes to mark the burials at the Little Big Horn?

7. What was Black Body better known as?

8. Captain Benteen said, "____ was just about as much cut out for a cavalryman as he was for a king."

9. Who said: "I'm going to war and so help me God, I'll not sheath my sword until that flag waves over the last revolted state"?

10. Custer's first official notification of appointment to the military academy bore the signature of ____.

11. Sitting Bull said that he had an arrow in his quiver for ____. They had hand-to-hand combat in the trading post at Ft. Berthold in 1868.

12. F Troop's Dennis Lynch stayed on the steamer Far West because he gave his horse to ____, at Custer's request.

13. Where was the wound Custer's horse Dandy suffered?

Answers to the annual quizzes start on page 41

14. Who was the last survivor of Custer's 7th Cavalry in the Sioux Campaign of 1876?

15. Who once wrote: "Thoughtlessness in regard to the safety of anything entrusted to my care, is a defect in my character, which I cannot correct"?

1997 - QUIZ NUMBER 18

Winner - Gary Gilbert of Cape Girardeau, Missouri

Authors - Dennis Farioli and Vincent Heier

1. What was the total number of horses and mules that left Ft. Lincoln on May 17, 1876?

2. Who was called "Count No Account?"

3. Who said, "As a soldier I would rather lie with the dead at the Battle of the Little Big Horn, than live with the survivors"?

4. Elihu F. Clear was the orderly of _____ at the Battle of the Little Big Horn.

5. What 7th Cavalry officer was superintendent of public schools of the city of Toledo, Ohio?

6. After the Civil War, Congress passed the Army Act of 1866, which reorganized the regular army and assigned it three missions. What were they?

7. The wife of Rear Admiral John C. Febiger was killed in a carriage accident 1n 1889. She was also the mother of what 7th Cavalry officer?

8. What did the Cheyenne call the Little Big Horn River?

9. On the fifth anniversary of the battle, Libbie Custer received a momento from Nelson Miles. What was it?

10. While several 7th Cavalry wore buckskins, only one officer of the Montana Column did. Who was this officer?

11. What is the name of the "well known military firm" where Custer purchased his lieutenants uniform?

12. Sioux Chief Red Cloud spoke the following eulogy about whom? "He, at least, never lied to us. His words gave the people hope. He died and their hope died again."

Answers to the annual quizzes start on page 41

13. Name the person who so impressed Custer on the 1873 Yellowstone Expedition because "has traversed more than 200 miles" alone and unarmed from Fort Rice?

14. Congressman John A. Bingham nominated George Custer to West Point. What 7th Cavalry officer was nominated by Congressman W. A. Richardson?

15. The remains of George Custer were ferried to West Point on a vessel named _____?

16. Which Indian casualty in the Battle of the Little Big Horn was "37 years old and left a widow and two daughters?"

17. How long did telegraph operator John M. Carnahan stay at his key to break the news of Custer's defeat to the East, and how did he retain possession of the line for further dispatches?

18. Mrs. Custer wrote an anguished appeal to this individual "not to permit any memorial of any kind" to Major Reno. Who was he and what was his connection to the Battlefield?

19. Name the two types of flowers which were used to adorn George Custer's casket?

20. The flag draped on Custer's casket was reportedly previously used on the casket of which other 7th Cavalry officer?

1998 - QUIZ NUMBER 19

Winners - Gary Gilbert of Cape Girardeau, Missouri
and
Dale Kosman of Lombard, Illinois
Authors - Dennis Farioli and Vincent Heier

1. Lincoln described him as "a chunky little chap, with a long body, short legs and not enough neck to hang him." Who was Lincoln describing?

2. Who resigned his commission to become a San Francisco banker?

3. His family called him "Cump." Who was he?

4. Fort Riley, named for Gen. Bennet Riley, was originally called Camp Center. Why?

5. Two Crow Indians got into a quarrel over a Sioux pony they found while with the Montana column. How did they settle their dispute?

Answers to the annual quizzes start on page 41

6. Which 7th Cavalry officer was sprayed by a skunk during the Washita Campaign?

7. What happened to Bloody Knife's horse after the scout was killed?

8. On June 29, 1876, which Republican congressman addressed the House of Representatives to urge the opening of the Black Hills for exploration and settlement?

9. Who were the first people to go back to the Custer Battlefield after June of 1876?

10. Who was the last participant of the Battle of the Little Big Horn to die?

11. What was the name of the steamer that transported the bodies of the 7th Cavalry officers disinterred by Col. Michael Sheridan in 1877?

12. What two 7th Cavalry companies had the highest rates of courts-martial prior to the Little Big Horn?

13. Custer graduated 34th in a class of 35 from West Point in 1861. Who failed to graduate?

14. Someone at the Little Big Horn had a grandfather who had been awarded medals from King George III for service to the crown in the War of 1812. Who was he?

15. Custer's famous "sailor shirt," which became a distinctive part of his Civil War attire, was supposedly a gift from whom?

16. Who should have been serving as the proper commander of Company E, 7th Cavalry at the Little Big Horn?

17. The Crows called Custer "Son of the Morning Star." The Rees called someone "Man in Calf Skin Vest." Who was he?

18. Who was believed to be the last surviving witness to the battle and when did he die?

19. When Ranald Mackenzie attacked Dull Knifes camp after the Little Big Horn, his troops found numerous items from Custer's ill-fated command, including the buckskin jacket of which officer?

20. Mark Kellogg was correspondent for the *Bismarck Tribune* on the 1876 Campaign with Custer. There was another who was to serve as a part-time reporter for the *New York Sun* but only got as far as the Powder River. Who was he?

Answers to the annual quizzes start on page 41

1999 - QUIZ NUMBER 20

Winners - Gary Gilbert of Cape Girardeau, Missouri

and

Dale Kosman of Lombard, Illinois

Authors - Dennis Farioli and Vincent Heier

1. Who served as commander of the newly formed 7th Cavalry until the arrival of Andrew Jackson Smith?

2. Who was the maternal grandfather of Captain Louis McClane Hamilton?

3. Captured by Confederates in June of 1863, this future 7th Cavalry officer spent two years as a prisoner of war in the notorious Andersonville and Charleston prisons. Who was he?

4. Who said: "I have seen the best cavalry regiments of England and did not think them equal to the Sioux as horsemen and shots"?-

5. Why were Nelson Miles' hopes for a peaceful end to the Sioux War thrown into quandary on December 16, 1876?

6. Why did Samuel J. Crawford resign his governor's office on November 4, 1868?

7. Post surgeon Doctor McGillycuddy was with him when he died. Who was he?

8. Lieutenant J. B. Rodman, regimental adjutant of the 20th Infantry, was stationed at Fort Snelling in Minnesota when he first heard the news of the Custer Battle. What was so strange about the news?

9. When was the last wild buffalo killed?

10. Until the arrival of the first superintendent in 1893, care for the Custer Battlefield National Cemetery was the responsibility of whom?

11. When 2nd Lt. G. A. Custer left West Point in July, 1861 he went to where in Washington, D.C.?

12. Two of Custer's West Point classmates sought and obtained commissions in what foreign country's army?

13. Captain George F. Price provided dates and military details for whose biographical sketch of Custer?

14. Which Custer-related film used the Anheuser Busch print in advertising and a press-book that advised, "Exploit it. June 25th is the 75th Anniversary of the Little Big Horn?"

Answers to the annual quizzes start on page 41

15. Which Seventh Cavalry trooper had the nickname, "Bounce?"

16. Captain McDougall recommended which two men of his company for the Medal of Honor, for recovery of Hodgson's body?

17. Why was it natural that when Reno attacked the village, he first encountered members of the Unkpapa band? (Hint: it's all in the name!)

18. What was a "hickory" shirt used by some troopers as an alternative to the regular army blouse?

19. Whose description of the Battle of the Little Big Horn was described by a Seventh Cavalry officer—himself a writer—as "by all accounts the most circumstantial, comprehensive, and straight forward"?

20. Which Indian, mistakenly thinking the Cheyenne, Bearded Man, who died in the battle was a scout, scalped. him and then later gave the scalp to the dead man's parents?

Answers to the annual quizzes start on page 41

Autie Reed and Friends
Harry J. Pareton, (left), George W. Godfray (center), and Autie Reed, right

1980 – ANSWERS TO QUIZ NUMBER 1

1. George A. Custer *(Old Neutriment)*

2. Tuck and Bleauch *(Old Neutriment)*

3. Two Moon *(Wooden Leg: A Warrior Who Fought Custer)*

4. George Wallace and Luther Hare *(Custer's Luck)*

5. Senator Wm. B. Allison. Iowa *(Red Cloud and the Sioux Problem)*

6. Elmer Otis *(Garryowen in Glory)*

7. Katherine Garrett and Capt. Myles Moylan *(With Custer's Cavalry)*

8. Fred Benteen, James Calhoun and Luther Hare *(Biographies of the Seventh Cavalry)*

9. Pvt. Archibald McIlharey and Pvt. John Mitchell *(Biographies of the Seventh Cavalry)*

10. Crowfoot *(Sitting Bull Champion of the Sioux)*

1981 – ANSWERS TO QUIZ NUMBER 2

1. Gall at Oak Creek, SD.

2. Jeremiah Finley *(Men with Custer, Hammer, p. 107.)*

3. Muggins Taylor & Henry Bostwick.

4. Richard Roberts

5. Bloody Knife, Bob-Tailed Bull & Little Brave (Little Soldier)

6. Minneconjous

7. Company G.

8. Myles Moylan *(Custer's Last Battle, p. 26)*

9. Company A

10. Thomas H. Laforge.

1982 – ANSWERS TO QUIZ NUMBER 3

1. *Josephine*

2. Alfred Terry

3. G. E. Smith, J. H. Meier, Roman Rutten or James Turley

4. George Wallace

5. Myles Keogh

6. Marcus A. Reno

7. E.S. Godfrey, although Miles Moylan is acceptable because he was also wounded

8. 42 or 45 depending on whose version you accept

9. White Swan

10. Southern Cheyenne

1983 - ANSWERS TO QUIZ NUMBER 4

1. Pvt. Lorentz

2. Lt. Benny Hodgeson

3. F. F. Girard

4. F. F. Girard

5. Lt. Charles Varnum

6. Lt. James H. Bradley

7. Wooden Leg

8. Lt. Luther Hare

9. Two Moon

10. Black Elk

1984 - ANSWERS TO QUIZ NUMBER 5

1. Wooden Leg
2. Edward S. Godfrey
3. Half Yellow Face (Big Belly
4. George A. Custer
5. George Wallace
6. Charles Windol.
7. Mitch Bouye
8. Charles Windolf
9. Marcus A. Reno
10. Mrs. Spotted Horn Bull

1985 - ANSWERS TO QUIZ NUMBER 6

1. *On the Little Big Horn* or *Custer's Last Stand*
2. Charles Dodae and Galusha Pennypacker
3. 1930
4. Marcus A. Reno and John J. Crittenden
5. Dewey Beard
6. Luther R. Hare or Charles Varnum
7. Goes Ahead
8. Richard E. Thompson
9. White-Man-Runs-Him
10. William Van Wyck Reily

1986 - ANSWERS TO QUIZ NUMBER 7

1. Black Shawl

2. Nelson A. Miles

3. Early 1930s

4. White-Man-Runs-Him

5. Thomas W. Custer, James Calhoun, Thomas French and Algernon Smith

6. Philip H. Sheridan

7. June 25, 1952

8. Usher L. Burdick

9. 1860

10. Lt. Godfrey

1987 - ANSWERS TO QUIZ NUMBER 8

1. Bob Davern

2. Gall

3. Lt. Edward J. McClernand

4. Wooden Leg

5. Medicine Tail Ford

6. 1917

7. Boston Custer, *sic.* Arthur Reed (Harry Armstrong Reed), Frank Mann, Mark Kellogg, Charlie Reynolds, Isaiah Dorman and Mitch Boyer

8. Mitch Boyer

9. 1932

10. Vehoenxne

1988 – ANSWERS TO QUIZ NUMBER 9

1. Comanche
2. Charlie Reynolds
3. Holmes O. Paulding
4. White Bull
5. Horace Countryman
6. Mary Holland
7. Kate Bighead
8. Edward S. Luce
9. Rain-in-the-Face
10. Red Horse

1989 - ANSWERS TO QUIZ NUMBER 10

1. Vincent Charlie

2. Sixteen

3. "No ne sapues sin raison: no me enbaines sine honor." (Draw me not without reason: sheath me not without honor.)

4. Fort Reno, Indian Territory (Oklahoma) and Fort Reno, Wyoming Territory. Neither was named for Marcus A. Reno. They were named for Jesse L. Reno

5. Jump

6. He urged the creation of the National Cemetery and submitted plans for the memorial shaft

7. Lt. Charles F. Roe

8. Edward Custer, July 25, 1882 to July 24, 1887

9. Samuel D. Sturgis

10. Sgt. George H. Geiger, Blacksmith Henry Mechlin, Saddler Otto Voit and Pvt. Charles Windolf

1990- ANSWERS TO QUIZ NUMBER

1. Elizabeth Custer

2. Marcus A. Reno

3. Benjamin Criswell, Charles Cunningham, Thomas Murray, Richard Hanley and Henry Holden

4. Dr. John Forsyth, West Point Chaplin

5. They broke the news of the battle to Elizabeth Custer.

6. Brave Bear

7. Sgt. Stanislaus Roy

8. $30.00 a month

9. 1938

10. Emanuel Custer

1991 - ANSWERS TO QUIZ NUMBER 12

1. Lydia Kirkpatrick Reed (Custer fell off a cow) *Crazy Horse and Custer p. 90*

2. Pvt. Byron L. Tarbox and Pvt. Wm. E. Morris, *Greasy Grass Vol. 2,1986 p. 4*

3. Low Dog- Oglala *(Custer Myth p. 75)*

4. Oscar Pardee, aka John Burke ("Custer's Last Stand Marine," *Real West June 1985, p. 26*)

5. Lt. Charles A. Varnum; February 26, 1936 *(Custer's Chief of Scouts p. 16-17)*

6. Paddie *(His Very Silence Speaks, p. 54-55)*

7. Long Road - Chauku Haysha, Sans Arc *(Warpath p. 203)*

8. Dr. James DeWolf *(They Rode With Custer)*

9. They were both wounded during the Battle of the Washita and killed at the Little Big Horn. *(Battle of Washita, p. 208-209, They rode With Custer)*

10. Pvt. William Wright, Co. C was 17 and Farrier Benjamin Brandon, Co. F was 45 *(They Rode With Custer)*

1992 - ANSWERS TO QUIZ NUMBER 13

1. Sgt. John Ryan Co. M and Capt. Thomas W. French Co., M.

2. *Annie Laurie, Little Footsteps Soft and Gentle, The Doxology, The Goodbye at the Door, and For He's a Jolly Good Fellow.*

3. Dog's Backbone: Sunku Chan Koha - Minneconjou

4. The Sioux Indian Battlefield

5. July 1929

6. Two, Corporal George H. King, July 1, 1876 and Pvt. William George, July 3, 1876.

7. Yellow Weasel

8. 1930

9. Capt. Frederick W. Benteen - June 26, 1876 - hilltop fight.

10. General E.R.S. Canby killed in 1873 during peace negotiations with Captain Jack and the Klamath Indians, Lava Beds, California and Lieutenant Colonel William H. Lewis, 19th Infantry

1993 ANSWERS TO QUIZ NUMBER 14

1. Frank Hunter

2. Sacristan

3. Answers follow:

1. Charlie Reynolds	E.	Lucky Man
2. Fred Gerard	D.	Seven Yanktons
3. Capt. Thomas French	F.	Tucker
4. Col. John Gibbon	C.	Chief with a red nose
5. Maj. Marcus A. Reno	B.	Man with dark face
6. Lt. George Wallace	I.	Nick
7. Bloody Knife	G.	Nes I Ri Pat
8. Lt. Col. G.A. Custer	J.	Ouches
9. Mitch Boyer	A.	Kapesh
10. Charles Varnum	H.	Crazy Horse

4. Joe Bush was a bulldog

5. Napoleon III

6. Rename it the Custer River

7. (a) J. Carrol Naish - (b) Sitting Bull (c) Rio Grande

8. 1839 and 1876 (the years Custer was born and died)

9. Myles Moylan

10. West Point, NY - 1879; Custer City, CO, - 1902

1994 - ANSWERS TO QUIZ NUMBER 15

1. Private Edward Davern (*Custer's Last Battle*, p. 15)

2. The New York Herald (*History of Custer Battlefield*, p. 69)

3. Circling Bear (*My Friend the Indian*, p.130)

4. David McWilliams (*They Rode With Custer*)

5. Elihu F. Clear (*Custer's Luck*, p. 377)

6. $13.00 a month plus longevity increases of $1.00 per month the 3rd year, $2.00 per month during the 4th year, and $3.00 per month the 5th year to be paid at discharge. (*Forty Miles a Day on Beans and Hay*, p. 127)

7. Edward Housen, Company D (*They Rode With Custer*)

8. White-Man-Runs-Him, Crow Scout (*Custer in '76*, p.178)

9. Captain Myles Moylan (*Reno Court of Inquiry*, p. 243)

10. 657

1995 - ANSWERS TO QUIZ NUMBER 16

1. Severe hernia (*Son of the Morning Star*, p. 41)

2. High Bear (*Arikara Narrative*, p. 74)

3. J.J. McGinnis (*Custer Battle Casualties*, p. 140)

4. John Stuart Forbes aka John S. Hiley (*They Rode with Custer*)

5. Myles Keough (*Time-Life Civil War Series-Gettysburg*, p. 46)

6. Lyman Kidder (*Court Martial of G.A. Custer*, p. 76)

7. April 4, 1838, March 20, 1891 (*The Actor and the General*)

8. George Herendeen (*1874 Invasion of Montana*)

9. Little Hawk (*Crazy Horse & Custer*, p. 219)

10. Elizabeth Custer (*General Custer's Libbie*)

11. Major Brisbin (*Keep the Last Bullet for Yourself*)

12. Andrew Nathan Glover, July 11,1893 (*History of Custer Battlefield*, p. 46)

13. Mitch Boyer (*Custer's Last Campaign*, p. 18)

14. Private John H. Tuttle (*Custer's 7th Cavalry and the Campaign of 1873*, p. 84)

15. Second Lieutenant Godfrey (*CBHMA 6th Annual Symposium,* p. 26)

1996- ANSWERS TO QUIZ NUMBER 17

1. September 6, 1876, under the command of Captain Weir [Major Reno turned over command on the 19th] (Nichols, *Reno Court of Inquiry*, "Introduction")

2. The trial of Captain French (Johnson, *A Captain of Chivalric Courage* p. 30)

3. Bloody Knife (Hammer, *Men With Custer*, p. 30)

4. Gustave Korn (Hammer, *Men With Custer*)

5. Lt. Kinzie (Carroll, *General Custer and the Battle of the Big Horn: The Federal View*, p. 42.)

6. James Campbell, civilian scout with Gibbon (Rickey, *History of Custer Battlefield*, p. 65)

.7. Lame Whiteman (Marquis, *Keep the Last Bullet for Yourself*, p. 159

8. Sergeant Martini (Graham, *Custer Myth,* p. 180)

9. Alfred Terry (Darling, *Sad and Terrible Blunder* p. 81)

10. Jefferson Davis (Hutton, *The Custer Reader*, p. 33)

11. Fred Gerard (Hammer, *Custer in '76*, p. .229)

12. George Herendeen (Hammer, *Custer in '76*, p. 221)

13. In the neck (Wagner, *Old Neutriment*, p. 151)

14. Jacob Horner (Ellison, *Sole Survivor*, p. 9)

15. Cadet, Marcus A. Reno (O'Neil, *Record of Demerits and Academics,* p. 26)

1997- ANSWERS TO QUIZ NUMBER 18

1. 1674 total horses and mules (*I Go With Custer*, p. 207)

2. Lt. DeRudio (*End of Custer*, p. 51)

3. Thomas Rosser (*Touched by Fire*, p. 309)

4. Lt. Hare (*End of Custer*, p. 118)

5. Joel Elliot (*The Custer Reader*, p. 178)

6. (a) reconstruction of the South (b) protection of the western frontier and (c) defense of the sea coasts (*Custer's First Sergeant John Ryan*, p. 87)

7. William Van Wyck Reily (*Greasy Grass*, Vol. 2)

8. The Goat River (*Custer in '76*, p. 212)

9. Map case carrier by Custer (*Cyclorama of Custer's Last Fight* p. 53)

10. Lt. "Johnny" McAdams, H Troop (*Custer Cavalry and Crows*, p. 77)

11. Horstman's in New York City (*The Custer Reader*, p. 46)

12. General George Crook (*Old West Quiz Fact Book*, p. 156)

13. Fr. Valentine Sommereisen (*Custer's 7th Cavalry and the Campaign of 1873*, p. 76.

14. Marcus Reno (*Reno Court of Inquiry - Abstract*, p. xxiv)

15. Mary Powell (*6th Annual CBHMA Symposium*, June, 26, 1992, p. 72)

16. Lame White Man *(Custer Reader*, p. 373)

17. Twenty-one hours - sent scripture passages from the New Testament (*Old West Quiz Fact Book*, p. 181)

18. J. A. Shoemaker, events coordinator for the 50th anniversary of the Little Bighorn *(Reno Court of Inquiry-Abstract*, p. xxiii)

19. Geraniums and tube roses (*6th Annual Symposium* of *CBHMA June, 26, 1992*, p. 72)

20. Captain Louis Hamilton (*6th Annual Symposium* of *CBHMA June, 26, 1992*, p. 72)

1998 - ANSWERS TO QUIZ NUMBER 19

1. Major General Phil Sheridan (*Cavalier in Buckskin*, p. 21)

2. William Tecumseh Sherman (*The Controversial Life of George Armstrong Custer*, p. 224)

3. William Tecumseh Sherman (*Heroes of The Civil War*, p. 96)

4. Because it was found to be very close to the geographical center of the USA (*Bugles Banners and Warbonnets*, p. 15)

5. They stabbed the pony to death. (*March of the Montana Column*, p. 95)

6. Tom Custer (*Greasy Grass*, Vol. 9)

7. To this day the Arikara people say that the horse returned to the village by itself, 500 miles, near present day Garrison, ND (*Greasy Grass*, Vol. 13)

8. Jefferson Kidder, father of Lyman Kidder (*Find Custer! The Kidder Tragedy*, p. 78)

9. Wooden Leg and five other Cheyenne a few months after the battle (*Son of the Morning Star*)

10. Dewey Beard sometimes, known as Iron Hail (*Son of the Morning Star*, p. 350)

11. *Fletcher. (The Custer Myth*, p. 375)

12. Companies B & G (*1996 CBHMA Symposium*, p. 20)

13. James P. Parker (*Unremaining Glory*)

14. Sitting Bull ("Sitting Bull and the Mounties," *Wild West* Feb. 1998, p. 33)

15. A gunboat crewman (*Custer and His Wolverines*, p. 131)

16. Charles Stillman Isley (*1993 CBHMA Symposium*, p. 14)

17. Mitch Boyer (*Little Big Horn Diary*, p. 221)

18. Charles Sitting Man 1962 (*Bloody Knife*, p. 170)

19. Tom Custer (*Mackenzie's Last Fight with the Cheyenne*, p. 30)

20. Richard Roberts (*1996 CBHMA Symposium*, p. 20)

1999 - ANSWERS TO QUIZ NUMBER 20

1. Major John W. Davidson of the 2nd Cavalry was in command until Smith took charge November 25, 1866. (*Cavalier in Buckskin*, p. 44)

2. Louis McClane, U. S. Senator and member of President Andrew Johnson's cabinet. (*Custer and the Battle of the Little Bighorn: An Encyclopedia*, p. 87)

3. Henry J. Nowlan. He escaped in February 1865 and joined Sherman's division. (*Custer and the Battle of the Little Bighorn: An Encyclopedia*, p. 133)

4. This was the assessment of Major J.M. Walsh, of the Northwest Mounted Police. Walsh told Nelson Miles that the Sioux holdouts could probably defeat the U.S. troops who had advanced to the border. (*Wolves for the Blue Soldiers*, p. 87)

5. Crow Scouts killed five Sioux leaders as they approached to inquire about terms for peace. (*Frontier Soldier*, p. 92)

6. To take command of the 19th Kansas Volunteers, as colonel of that regiment and join Sheridan's expedition at Camp Supply as the 7th Cavalry moved toward the Washita. (*Battle of the Washita*, p. 102)

7. Crazy Horse died from a bayonet wound at Fort Robinson, Nebraska on September 5, 1877 at 2 p.m. (*Killing of Chief Crazy Horse*, p. 95)

8. He heard it from an old Sioux, on July 3, 1876, before the *Far West* had started back with the wounded. (*With Custer on the Little Bighorn*, p. 114)

9. October 1890 in Oklahoma. The northern herds were wiped out by 1884 and the southern herds in 1887. (*Encyclopedia of the American West*, p. 53)

10. The post commander and his quartermaster officer at Fort Custer (*History of the Custer Battlefield*, p. 46)

11. Ebbit House (*Complete Life of Maj. Gen. George A. Custer*, p. 49)

12. Egyptian army (*Complete Life of Maj. Gen. George A. Custer*, p. 50)

13. Elizabeth Custer (*Tenting on the Plains*, p. 25)

14. *Little Big Horn (The Fighting Seventh)* (*Custer's Last Stand.- The Anatomy of an American Myth*, p. 107)

15. Henry Fisher (*4th Annual Symposium*, p. 9)

16. Sgt. Benjamin C. Criswell & Pvt. Stephen L. Ryan (*4th Annual Symposium*, p. 11)

17. Unkpapa is derived from the word meaning "open to camp." (*A Guide to the Indian Wars of the West*, p. 67)

18. A black and white checkered shirt (*A Guide to the Indian Wars of the West*, p. 37)

19. Mrs. Spotted Horn Bull (*Custer's Last Battle*, p. 1)

20. Little Crow (*The Custer Reader*, p. 342)

Answers to the annual quizzes start on page 41

INTRODUCTION TO
TRIVIA AND FACTS

Dennis Farioli

In the summer of 1997, I began writing the first pages of this book. It occurred to me that there are numerous facts and bits of information which are either unknown or overlooked. I began to keep a list of those items of trivia and facts which held my interest the most. As my collection grew, I realized this collection of information could be turned into an interesting book. I contacted The Rev. Vincent Heier, (Vince to me) and discussed the idea of putting these facts together in the form a book. Not only did Vince think this was a great idea, he also said he would like to contribute items from his vast collection of photos, poems, recordings and other Custer ephemera. The next step was to contact my friend, Tom Pream, who had served as CBHMA president before I took office. Tom also supported the idea of a Custer related quiz and trivia book and said he would collect an entire set of the annual CBHMA quizzes and their answers for this book.

At the annual board of director's meeting in June of 1998, I proposed to the board that CBHMA finance the publishing of this quiz and trivia book and in return the authors and editor would donate their time and efforts to prepare this book for publication in June of 1999. The proceeds will be donated to CBHMA.

At this time, I engaged the services of Nora Whitley, editor of our quarterly newsletter, *The Battlefield Dispatch*, to serve as editor of this joint project. Not only did Nora serve as editor, but she has written the preface and introduction. With all of the authors and editor organized, we then called upon Old Army Press of Fort Collins, Colorado and our friends, Mike and Dee Koury, to help us publish and print our quiz and trivia book. But what would we call it? All were agreed "Custer" had to appear in the title. After a two week debate, Tom Pream came up with the title of our project, *You Don't Know G.A. C.*, (pronounced Jack). The following is the result of the team effort of Vince Heier, Tom Pream, Nora Whitley and myself, with the generous help from our friends at Old Army Press. So read on, I am certain you will learn a few facts and gain insight into the fascinating subject of G.A.C. Who knows, you may find out *You Don't Know G.A.C.*

Dennis Farioli,
E. Longmeadow, MA
May 1999

Answers to Trivia & Facts start on page 111.

EARLY YEARS

1. Who was Matilda Viers?

2. Who was Israel Kirkpatrick?

3. Was George Armstrong the first child born to Emanuel and Maria Custer?

4. After whom was George Armstrong Custer named?

5. What was Armstrong's connection to Joseph R. Hunter?

6. What profession did Custer's mother hope he would take up?

7. After securing his teaching certificate from Harrison County Board of School Examiners, where did Custer teach?

8. Where did the River Raisin Massacre of 1813 occur?

9. In 1856, Autie earned $28 a month teaching school. He also earned an extra $2 a month. How did he earn it?

10. Who said, referring to G. A. Custer, "What a pretty girl he would have made"?

11. Who was the first of Custer's ancestors to reach this continent?

☆   FACT   ☆

George Armstrong Custer was born December 5, 1839, in New Rumley, Ohio. Once Anthony Wayne defeated Indian tribes in the mid-1790s, Ohio became the new magnet, with its promise of virgin land and the hope of a new beginning. Jacob Custer, Emanuel's uncle, stopped at a tiny settlement, Rumley Town, founded by a squatter, John Rumley. The village lay eleven miles from Cadiz and was re-christened New Rumley, (Custer: The Controversial Life of George Armstrong Custer, *p. 14).*

Answers to Trivia & Facts start on page 111.

WEST POINT

1. What year was West Point Military Academy founded?

2. On August 29, 1859, Custer was admitted to the post hospital at West Point for what problem?

3. What was Custer s best subject in his final year at West Point?

4. Custer graduated last in his class at West Point. Who graduated first?

5. In Custer's day at West Point, what were the lowest ranking members of a class referred to as?

☆   *FACT*   ☆

It is always pointed out that Custer finished last in his class at West Point, thirty-fourth in a class of thirty-four. Of one-hundred-eight potential students, only sixty-eight passed the entrance examination in 1857. After the completion of Custer's first term, eight more members of his class were dropped. Two years later, only thirty-five of those sixty remained. The course of studies was so rigorous that only those with outstanding ability or excellent preparation could stay in school. Custer stayed and Custer graduated! (Touched by Fire, p. 14).

6. Who described Custer as "a ladies' man of the love 'em and leave 'em variety?"

7. Custer accumulated 741 demerits while at West Point. How many offenses did he commit to earn this many?

8. A cadet could be dismissed when he acquired how many demerits?

9. Custer graduated from West Point in four years, one year early. Why?

Answers to Trivia & Facts start on page 111.

10. On what date did Custer graduate?

11. Who requested Custer be court-martialed for not stopping a fight, while he was officer of the guard at West Point?

12. Who were the two cadets involved in the fight?

13. Custer was charged with what?

14. What was engraved on Custer's West Point ring?

15. What West Point graduate was delayed by a one-year suspension for threatening an upper classman with a bayonet.?

16. What position did Custer apply for in 1869?

CIVIL WAR

1. George Armstrong Custer, "the boy general," was not the youngest of the Civil War generals. Who was?

2. One of Custer's rivals during the Civil War was John Singleton Mosby. What did he do before the war?

3. On December 13, 1862, which future 7th Cavalry officer was wounded when a Confederate shell exploded beneath his horse at Fredricksburg?

4. When did Custer first meet George Yates?

5. Who married George Yates on January 5, 1865?

6. Whose granddaughter was Gloria Vanderbilt?

7. On June 28, 1863, Custer received his promotion from captain to brevet brigadier general. Who were the other two of Pleasonton's captains to get their stars the same day?

8. What tune was always a signal for a charge for Custer's Wolverines?

9. In a December 29, 1863 letter to Custer, Libbie wrote, "God cure you of it." Cure him of what?

Answers to Trivia & Facts start on page 111.

Custer - early in his career

Photo courtesy of Little Bighorn Battlefield National Monument

10. Lincoln described him as a "brown chunky little chap, with a long body, short legs, and not enough neck to hang him." Who was Lincoln describing?

11. What was the first action Custer saw as a division commander?

12. Who commanded the Confederate's Laurel Brigade?

13. The battle of Tom's Brook became known as what?

14. In October of 1864, Custer and thirteen troopers went to Washington to present what to the secretary of war?

15. Who told Custer, "General, a gallant officer always makes gallant soldiers"?

16. Tom Custer captured two Confederate flags. Where did he do this?

17. Who said, "I hope the first God damned bullet gets you"?

18. Professor T.S.C. Lowe was one of Custer's instructors, but not at West Point. Where then?

☆   FACT   ☆

In 1861, Col. Hiram Burdan conceived the idea of forming special regiments of outstanding marksmen. Men first brought their own rifles, but as this created a problem of ammunition supply, Burdan requested Sharps rifles. After witnessing a spectacular exhibition of marksmanship, President Lincoln intervened and Sharps were issued to Burdan's regiment and later to others. Hence, the birth of "Sharpshooters," (Civil War Dictionary, p. 736).

19. What was different about Custer's uniform on December 25, 1865?

20. Mortally wounded at Cedar Creek, what Confederate friend of Custer's died at Sheridan's headquarters in Winchester?

Answers to Trivia & Facts start on page 111.

Lawrence Barrett. Photo courtesy of Dennis Farioli.

☆ FACT ☆

Libbie Custer reports her husband sat in the company of his actor friend, Lawrence Barrett, in Barrett's dressing room for forty consecutive nights during a long break of the play Julius Caesar. Each night after the long break, Custer would return to the audience to watch his friend "with unflagging interest." (Boots and Saddles, p. 250)

☆ FACT ☆

Famed actor of his day, Lawrence Barrett was a close friend of General George Armstrong Custer. Barrett was born April 4, 1838, in Paterson, New Jersey. He started his acting career at the age of 15 and made his first New York appearance in the Hunchback, as Sir Thomas Clifford, January 20, 1857.

During the Civil War, Barrett served as captain of Company B in the 28th Massachusetts Regiment from October 8, 1861 through August 8, 1862.

Barrett donated $250 toward the erection of a statue over Custer's grave and it was Mrs. Barrett who accompanied Libbie Custer on October 10, 1877 when Custer was laid to rest at West Point.

Barrett's repertory included all of the standard plays of his day, but he was best known for his portrayal of the Roman hero Cassius. During a performance of Richelieu at the Broadway Theater on March 18, 1891, Barrett became too ill to continue. Two days later he died in his apartment at the Windsor Hotel. He was buried in Cohasett, Massachusetts, where he had made his summer home for many years.

From The Actor and the General *by Alice T. O'Neil*

Answers to Trivia & Facts start on page 111.

21. Who was given the nickname "Savior of the Valley?"

22. Upon his first exposure to liberated negroes who said, "They will accept their freedom if offered to them, they will not of their own accord fight for it"?

23. Who said, "I have never in my life taken a command into battle and had the slightest desire to come out alive unless I won"?

24. After he graduated, what did Custer purchase in New York City?

25. Who was called "The Queen of Sheba?"

26. On January 27, 1864, Custer told brigade officers "I'm going out to the Department of the West to get a command, or a new commander." What did he mean?

27. At Trevilian Station, two people close to Custer were captured by Confederates. Who were they?

28. On April 9, 1865, Confederate Major Robert Sims, carrying a white towel, was escorted to Custer. What was his mission?

29. Who resigned his commission to become a San Francisco banker?

30. The Appomattox Campaign lasted from March 29 - April 9, 1865 before General Lee made his initial surrender to General Custer. What was Lee attempting to do there?

31. The artillery used something referred to as canister. What was canister?

32. What was the official name of the Confederate army?

33. What was the Confederate debt?

34. K.I.A. is killed in action. What is D.O.W.?

35. What was "hot shot?"

36. Who was the assistant instructor of infantry tactics at the USMA in the fall of 1865?

Answers to Trivia & Facts start on page 111.

BLUE COATS

1. During the Indian War period, three major recruit depots were maintained. Where were they?

2. How many companies composed a regiment in the regular army?

3. What was called the "curse of the army?"

☆   *FACT*   ☆

Secretary of War, Stephen B. Elkins, reported one-third of the men recruited between 1867 and 1891 had deserted. (ibid p. 143).

4. What was the average weight of a cavalry soldier?

5. What was a soldiers forage cap called?

6. What was the average age for a first time enlistment?

7. Captain John Bourke, a member of Crook's staff for sixteen years, thought the Indian Wars could have been shortened or even avoided. In what way?

8. How did General Sully refer to the Dakota Bad Lands?

9. If Custer was prohibited from directing the overall expedition in 1876, whom did Terry suggest to Sheridan?

10. Whose family referred to him as Cump?

☆   *FACT*   ☆

William Spencer McCaskey, who commanded Fort Lincoln in Custer's absence, was a captain in the 20th Infantry. He enlisted in the 79th Pennsylvania in 1861, as a private and retired in 1907 as a major general.

Answers to Trivia & Facts start on page 111.

William Spencer McCaskey, circa 1877. Photo courtesy of Hank Chapman.

☆   Fact   ☆

Records indicate that between 1865 and 1874 one-half of the enlisted personnel were foreign born. Of this figure, natives of Ireland and Germany accounted for the majority, (Custer: The Controversial Life of George Armstrong Custer, p. 246).

Answers to Trivia & Facts start on page 111.

ARMY SLANG

1. At camp or a garrison, what was walking the ring?

2. What was a whiskey soak?

3. What was nooning?

4. What was a shavetail?

5. What was a wind-sucker?

6. What was the grand bounce?

7. What was a wrangle?

8. What were Beecher's scouts?

9. What was a "Telegraph Smith" or "John?"

10. What was a Jenny Lind steak"

11. What was walking draft?

12. What was coffin varnish?

13. What was an I. C. brand?

14. What were old bummers?

15. Who was the hard crowd?

16. What was a G.C.M.?

17. What was "to show the white feather?"

18. What was Uncle Sam's seed cakes?

19. What was a top-knot?

20. What was skalljaw?

21. What was a coffee cooler?

22. What was goose wine?

23. What was a dog robber?

24. What was a windjammer?

25. What was a slum burner?

Answers to Trivia & Facts start on page 111.

26. What was a snow bird?

27. Who was Mr. Lo?

28. What was "to be dron out"?

29. What was old file?

FORTS

1. Fort Riley, named in honor of General Bennet Riley, was originally called "Camp Center." Why?

2. 270 feet above Fort Lincoln was a sister garrison first occupied by infantry in the summer of 1872. What was the post called?

3. For what purpose was Fort Lincoln constructed?

4. What fort was located on the Sun River?

5. Who was that fort's first commander?

6. What was the only fort named for an individual Indian?

7. The 7th Cavalry Headquarters was Fort Lincoln until June 1882. Then where was the 7th transferred?

8. What happened at Fort Robinson October 29, 1876?

9. What became of Thomas Newcomb?

10. Who built Fort Keogh?

11. After Sitting Bull crossed into Canada, what fort was constructed near the Canadian border?

12. What post did Custer refer to as "the lowest post he had ever known"?

13. What was the Sioux phrase for forts?

14. What was the abbreviation for commanding officer's wife?

15. Where and when did Alfred Terry meet George Custer?

16. Who built Fort Lincoln?

Answers to Trivia & Facts start on page 111.

CRITTERS 'N SUCH

1. Custer brought two dogs to Fort Riley. What were their names?

2. Indians killed Custer's dog at the Washita. What was the name of the dog?

3. How fast does a cavalry horse walk, trot and gallop?

4. Private William Baker filed a claim for his horse, killed in the Valley Fight. Why was the claim disallowed?

Capt. Weir's horse, circa 1875.
Photo courtesy of Little Bighorn Battlefield National Monument.

5. Two Crow Indians got into a quarrel over a Sioux pony they found while with the Montana Column. How did they settle the dispute?

6. Reno sent Lt. Hare for the packs, but first he traded horses with Lt. Godfrey. Why the trade?

Answers to Trivia & Facts start on page 111.

7. How long did it take Lt. Hare to get from Reno Hill to the pack train and back?

8. How many rounds of ammunition were carried by the pack mules?

9. Near the divide, Lt. Cooke came to Lt. Mathey with an order from Custer. What was the order?

10. Who first told Sergeant John Martin that his horse was wounded?

11. While hiding in the timber, Girard's horse began to whinny. Jackson did something to make him stop. What did he do?

12. What chore was given to Stanislas Roy, June 28, 1876?

13. While on Reno Hill, "Old Barnum" tried to charge the Indians by himself. What happened to him?

14. Each trooper carried 12 pounds of oats and two of something else. What?

15. On June 27, Herendeen found a dead horse in the river. What did he find under the horse?

16. At the divide, why did Mark Kellogg borrow spurs from Fred Girard?

17. Captain Benteen counted seventy dead horses after the battle. How many dead Indian ponies?

18. Armed only with a bowie knife, what one-time scout survived a bear attack?

19. On the Black Hills Expedition, Custer caught rattlesnakes, a badger, a porcupine, two marsh hawks and a jack rabbit. What did he do with them?

20. What did Custer keep in an inkwell on his desk?

21. Who was the veterinarian with the Dakota Column?

22. What officer was in charge of the pack train during the night march before the battle?

Answers to Trivia & Facts start on page 111.

23. Lt. James M. Burns, 17th Infantry, wrote Libbie Custer on August 19, 1876 and informed her that he had something she wanted. What?

24. How many fleas did Alfred Terry's dog Gyp have? No, really!

25. What did Phil Sheridan refer to as the "Indian's commissary?"

26. On his twenty-first birthday, what did the Grand Duke Alexis do with "Lucretia Borgia?"

27. Can you name the horse Custer rode to war in 1861?

28. Whose would-be wife killed two buffalo in July of 1870?

29. What officer was sprayed by a skunk during the Washita Campaign?

30. What happened to Bloody Knife's horse after he was killed?

31. What was significant about Major James Walsh's horse?

32. While fighting the Nez Perce at Bear Paw Mountain, Godfrey's mount was shot from under him. Where did he get the horse?

33. Forty-one cavalry recruits joined the army April 3, 1868, in St. Louis. Shortly thereafter they were sent to join the 7th Cavalry, then stationed in the field in Kansas. Who was the famous one?

34. What town was named in 1908 for a member of the 7th Cavalry?

35. Comanche survived the Custer Battle. Can you name the only living horse found after the Fetterman Fight?

36. What horse remains were preserved and now stand on display at the Smithsonian?

37. What did "Fox" and "Kangaroo" have in common with, "Cincinnati" and "Jeff Davis?"

38. In 1872, G.A. Custer purchased two race horses while in Elizabethtown. What were their names?

Answers to Trivia & Facts start on page 111.

☆   FACT   ☆

Beside his famous mount Traveller, Robert E. Lee's other horses were Richmond, Ajax and Lucy Long. William T Sherman owned Sam and Lexington. Phil Sheridan owned Rienzi (later changed to Winchester) and George B. McClellan's horses were Burns and Daniel Webster. (ibid p. 411).

POLITICS

1. On June 29, 1876, a republican congressman, addressed the House of Representatives to urge the opening of Black Hills for exploration and settlement. Who was the congressman?

2. Custer first testified before a house committee, March 29, 1876, under Hyster Clymer. Who was Clymer's roommate at Princeton College?

3. What did President Grant announce on May 29, 1876?

4. For whom was Bismarck, North Dakota, named?

5. The Army Act of July 28, 1866, authorized a regular army of how many?

6. In 1874 and 1875, Custer was involved in a media feud, a newspaper war. Who was Custer's opponent?

7. J.D. Thompson was really Ralph Meeker and Custer knew it. What was this all about?

☆   FACT   ☆

Most of Custer's testimony before the Clymer Committee was hearsay and would not have held up in a court of law. But this was not a court of law and most of what he said found corroboration in the testimony of others (ibid p. 159).

Answers to Trivia & Facts start on page 111.

8. Herbert Hoover appointed the daughter of a 7th Cavalry officer postmistress at West Point. Who was her father?

9. In May of 1876, Grant appointed his third secretary of war, James Don Cameron. What was his military background?

10. It was hoped that something would be issued to publicize the 50th anniversary of the Custer battle. What something?

11. Emanuel Custer visited his son's widow in New York in 1876. He told Libbie he would not go home without first seeing somebody. Whom did he wish to see?

☆ FACT ☆

Beside the post tradership scandal that led to a congressional investigation, Grant was also troubled by the whiskey ring scandal, a conspiracy to divert large sums of whiskey tax money into the pockets of Grant's friend, John McDonald and Grant's secretary, Orville Babcock. In addition to these was the Credit Mobilier fraud, which had charged the public 94 million dollars for railroad track that cost only 44 million. It was no wonder Grant did not seek a third term (ibid p. 255).

12. What act, passed in 1887, allotted 160 acres of Crow land to each head of household?

☆ FACT ☆

The New York Stock Exchange closed after the collapse of Jay Cooke Co., a financial firm, as well as several banks. The Northern Pacific Railroad declared bankruptcy. All were contributing factors that led to the Panic of 1873, (Custer: The Controversial Life of George Armstrong Custer, p. 310).

Answers to Trivia & Facts start on page 111.

RIVERS & BOATS

Steamboat Rosebud, *circa unknown.*
Photo courtesy of Little Bighorn Battlefield National Monument.

1. The first camp en route to the Little Big Horn was at the Heart River and it was there the men were paid. Who was the paymaster?

2. At the mouth of the Tongue River was an abandoned Indian camp. What did Custer find there?

3. What officer was in charge of the steamboat *Far West*?

4. Between the bow and the stern of the *Far West* was a wide open space. How was this space utilized?

5. The hospital area of the *Far West* had the floor covered with something. What was it?

6. The surgeon on board the *Far West* declared it, "The best field hospital he had ever seen." Who was the surgeon?

Answers to Trivia & Facts start on page 111.

7. Referring to the boat ride back to Fort Lincoln, who called it, "the lightning steamboat ride?"

8. Who were the riverboat pilots on board the *Far West?*

9. The speed of the *Far West* on the return trip to Fort Lincoln was unrivaled in the annals of boating. What was the speed of the *Far West?*

10. Who was the post trader who went as far as the Heart River?

11. What were the Arikara names for the following rivers: Missouri, Little Missouri, Yellowstone, Powder and Rosebud?

12. Who commanded the Powder River Depot?

13. What was the steamer that took the remains of the officers back the following year?

14. In what capacity did James Sipes serve on board the *Far West?*

15. Why was there a need to run pumps on the *Far West?*

16. The men at the Powder River piled up wood for what reason?

17. What are the chief tributaries of the Yellowstone River?

18. What were the two steamers the army chartered for the Yellowstone Expedition in 1873?

19. What was the name of the steamboat that brought Sitting Bull and his followers to Standing Rock?

20. Sitting Bull wore something strange on the steamboat. What was he wearing?

21. In 1882, Grant Marsh, now skipper of the *W.F. Behan*, noted an amusing peculiarity about Indians. What was it about them he thought was so funny?

22. What alarmed Custer the evening of the first camp at the Heart River?

Answers to Trivia & Facts start on page 111.

☆   FACT   ☆

The Far West was constructed at Pittsburgh, PA, in 1870, by the Coulson brothers boat building firm. It was 190 feet long, 33 feet across her lower deck and had a storage capacity of 400 tons. Her engine was built by Herbertson Engine Works of Brownsville, PA, and her crew numbered thirty (ibid p. 51).

23. What was the Pioneer Battalion?

24. What was said to be "too thick to drink and too thin to plow?"

25. What happened June 12, 1876, at Stanley's Stockade?

☆   FACT   ☆

Boston Custer had taken considerable interest in learning the skills of piloting a steamboat. So much so, that by June 22, he almost decided to forego accompanying his brothers on the pursuit of the Indians (ibid p. 213).

26. Who was in charge of the steamboat, *Josephine*?

27. After whom was the steamer *Josephine* named?

Answers to Trivia & Facts start on page 111.

SCOUTS

1. Indian scouts refused to carry the mail to Fort Laramie through Indian country during the Black Hills expedition. Who did?

2. The Arikara scouts earned extra money while traveling to the Little Big Horn. How did they do it?

3. How many Ree scouts were killed in the Valley Fight?

4. Isaiah Dorman, a Negro interpreter employed at Ft. Rice, was finally killed by whom?

5. Mitch Boyer's father was killed by Indians. What became of his brother John?

6. Who ripped open the lone tepee?

7. When leaving the timber, Herendeen told a group of soldiers with him not to run, but to go in skirmish order, take it cool, don't shoot unless necessary and we could get out. A wounded sergeant with them said: "I will shoot the first man to disobey." Who was the sergeant?

8. Who was known to the Indians as "Swift Buffalo?"

9. "It occurred to me then and I am still of the same opinion, that the timber was a splendid place for defense and Reno made a terrible blunder in not remaining there." Who said these words?

10. Of all the Crow scouts with Custer, who was in charge?

11. Who said the charge of abandonment of Major Elliott at the Washita was made by Captain Benteen because "he was anxious to weaken Custer's prestige"?

12. Who discovered the fate of Lt. Lyman Kidder?

13. Who rode for the Pony Express at age 14?

14. Who was awarded the Congressional Medal of Honor in 1872, only to have it revoked 44 years later?

Answers to Trivia & Facts start on page 111.

15. Who was the Osage scout who told Custer, referring to the Washita village, "Heap Injuns down there"?

16. At the Washita, who rode beside Custer in the charge?

17. Who was Bloody Knife's wife?

18. Five years after Bloody Knife's death, his widow received something from the United States government. What did she receive?

19. Isaiah Dorman was owed $62.50 for his services that summer. Who collected his wages?

20. Who hugged his horse and said "I love you," then stood up and began shooting?

21. In camp on May 30, 1876, why did Robert Jackson stand on a water keg with just one foot?

22. Why was Lt. Varnum watching Charlie Reynolds rather than the Indians?

23. On his way to Deadwood, Wild Bill Hickok and his party stopped briefly at the ranch of John Hunton. Shortly after they departed, Hickok sent word back to Hunton that he forgot something and wanted it sent to him in Deadwood. What was the article?

24. Who was called the "poet scout?"

25. Thomas H. LeForge, in addition to his scouting pay, was paid an extra dollar a day. By whom?

26. The Crows gave him the cherished rank of "Wolf." Who held this honor?

27. From June 9 on, Tom LeForge was of no use to Bradley as a scout. Why not?

28. What Crow Indian with the Montana Column was nicknamed "the Senator?"

29. Gibbon said, "He was the only half breed I ever met who could give the distances to be covered with accuracy, in miles." To whom was he referring?

Answers to Trivia & Facts start on page 111.

30. "If the Sioux kill me, I have the satisfaction of knowing I popped many of them over and they can't get even now, if they do get me." Who made this statement?

31. On June 29 at the Powder River Depot, Major Orlando H. Moore received news of the disaster from scout Charlie Cross and two Ree scouts. What was his response?

32. The Crow scout, Curley, had only one child. What was her name?

33. Curley's son-in-law, Dominic Old Elk, remarried and left Curley to raise a young boy. For whom was the child named?

MONTANA COLUMN

1. A white man with a long gray beard and dressed liked an Indian was found in a tree, dead, by one of Gibbon's men. He had five or six bullet wounds. Who found him?

2. On June 27, 1876, Captain Benteen was escorted to the Custer Battlefield. Who was his guide?

3. What attracted Lt. Bradley and his mounted infantry to the Custer Battlefield?

4. On June 26, 1876, three Crow scouts who had been with Custer, attempted to communicate with a series of cries. Who explained to Bradley that they were songs for mourning the dead?

5. Who was the Crow scout, with Bradley, to whom the three Crows told the story to?

6. Three men from the 2nd Cavalry went hunting May 23, 1876. What happened?

7. Who were the three men from the 2nd Cavalry who went hunting?

8. In the Montana Column, who was the sub-commander of the infantry segment?

Answers to Trivia & Facts start on page 111.

9. Who wrote, "It is understood, that if Custer arrives first, he is at liberty to attack at once, if he deems prudent"?

10. Name the two men Terry sent to unite with Custer, as the Montana Column made its approach to the valley of the Little Big Horn.

11. Who in the Montana Column caught an antelope alive?

12. What were Dr. Paulding's feelings toward Gibbon?

WYOMING COLUMN

1. Who said: "The worse it gets, the better. Always hunt Indians in bad weather"?

2. While on his scout up the Rosebud, had Reno learned of Crook's situation June 17, 1876, could Reno have ridden to Crook's aid?

3. When Sheridan learned of Crook's discontinued efforts in the field, he sent Crook a telegram, via Fort Fetterman. What did Sheridan tell Crook?

✫ FACT ✫

While Crook camped along the upper waters of Goose Creek, June 25, 1876. Captain Anson Mills, Lt. Frederick Schwatka and their small party explored the high country to the north and west. Mills later recalled, "I observed a great smoke to the northwest." Correspondent John Finerty would later write, "It was a prairie fire sure enough, but it was kindled by the deadly, far sweeping musketry of the vengeful savages, who annihilated Custer." (ibid p. 324).

4. During the Rogue River War in Oregon, George Crook received what wound?

5. "Every lodge will send its young men and they will say of the great father's dogs, 'let them come.'" Who spoke these words?

Answers to Trivia & Facts start on page 111.

6. Who was in charge of Crook's cavalry?

7 Who commanded Crook's infantry?

8. Who was called the "Irish Pencil Pusher?"

9. When did Crook depart from Fort Fetterman?

10. Captain Van Vliet and Company G, left Fort Fetterman one day in advance of Crook. Why?

11. On June 14, 1876, what brought cheers to Crook's men?

12. What was the total number of Crook's Indian Scouts?

13. What was the total number in manpower, in Crook's strike force?

14. Crook's was the largest command since 1865. Who had a larger command in 1865?

15. How did the Cheyenne refer to the Rosebud Battle?

☆   *FACT*   ☆

Eight months after the Rosebud Battle, General Sherman, wrote to General Sheridan "Crook should not have abandoned the field. Instead of moving back his train, he should have brought his train up to him and kept up the pressure and had he done so, the Custer Massacre was an impossibility. This in my judgment, was a terrible mistake and I cannot shut my eyes and understanding to it." (Touched By Fire. p. 282).

16. How did Crook's men distinguish between the enemy and allied Indian Scouts?

17. How many soldiers were killed at the Rosebud Battle?

18. Who was the only officer at the Rosebud Battle who had received a Medal of Honor during the Civil War?

Answers to Trivia & Facts start on page 111.

☆ *FACT* ☆

Slim Kobold owned much of the land encompassing the Rosebud Battlefield and it was officially dedicated in 1934. Millions of tons of coal lay just beneath the surface of the ground. Mr. Kobold could have easily sold out to mining developers, but he wanted the battlefield preserved. In 1972, the Rosebud Battlefield was placed on the National Register of Historic Places. While dying of cancer, Mr. Kobold purchased the land from his hospital bed in Billings and signed the papers in 1978, making the Rosebud Battlefield a state monument, (ibid).

CHEYENNE & SIOUX

☆ *FACT* ☆

The Ojibwa word for "group" rendered into French by early explorers and traders as Nadouessioux was shortened to Sioux and passed into English, (ibid).

1. What did the Indians call the Wolf Mountains?

2. Why was White Bull, a Minneconjou warrior, appalled at the death of Lame White Man, the brave Cheyenne leader?

3. Who said, referring to Sitting Bull, "If someone would lend him a heart, he would fight?"

4. Why did warriors under Crazy Horse became impatient with him when the fighting started?

5. On June 20, 1876, Captain Pollock telegraphed the department commander from Fort Laramie. Why?

6. What was a "Dog Soldier?"

7. At what age did the Sioux give up aggressive warrior activity?

8. The Cheyenne warrior society had one major chief. How many subsidiary chiefs or little chiefs were in a warrior society?

Answers to Trivia & Facts start on page 111.

9. A chief in a warrior society was not a commander. What was he?

10. Separating from Crazy Horse and Sitting Bull after the battle, this Oglala chief was leading his people to the agency. At Slim Buttes, he and several of his followers were killed by Crook's troops. Who was he?

11. What Hunkpapa leader was a life long enemy of the Arikara scout Bloody Knife?

12. In a joint effort, what did Red Tomahawk and Bullhead do?

13. What Oglala warrior made it a point to never take a scalp?

14. Who was the army private who is generally credited as the killer of Crazy Horse?

15. What did Crow Dog do August 5, 1881?

16. What Indian attended official events on the reservation in a business suit?

17. What Indian veteran of the Custer Battle was one of three models for the Indian head nickel?

18. What was Sitting Bull's childhood name?

19. On January 15, 1891, this veteran of the Custer Battle gave up his rifle to Nelson Miles, which is significant to history as the last formal subjugation of Native Americans by the U.S. Army. Who was he?

20. Who did Stanley Vestal claim was the killer of Custer?

21. A Cheyenne warrior, Brave Bear, was elected to the highly honorable status of what?

22. Rain-in-the-Face was arraigned in federal court. With what was he charged?

23. Minnie Hollow Wood, a Sioux woman, was the only woman at the time entitled to do what?

24. Where and when was Sitting Bull born?

25. Who introduced the Ghost Dance?

Answers to Trivia & Facts start on page 111.

26 Lakota or Dakota, means what?

☆   FACT   ☆

The Sioux fought on the side of the British during the War of 1812. (ibid)

27. What are the three major divisions of Sioux?

28. What rival tribe forced the Sioux west to the plains?

☆   FACT   ☆

The basic unit of the Sioux was the "tiyospe," an extended family group, that traveled together in search of game.

29. During the Black Hills expedition, of 1874, Custer surprised five lodges of Sioux (27 people). Who was chief?

30. Sitting Bull, with 186 of his followers, surrendered July 20, 1881, at Fort Buford. He turned his rifle over to whom?

☆   FACT   ☆

In 1880, a delegation of Sioux. ventured across the Canadian border, for a visit with "Bearcoat" Miles. Miles demonstrated the telephone and, when they recognized voices of distant friends speaking the Dakota language, "huge drops of perspiration coursed down their bronze faces and with trembling hands, they laid the instrument down." After this they became advocates of peace. (ibid p. 18).

31. Sitting Bull charged from twenty-five cents to two dollars for it, but he never charged a woman for it. What was he selling?

Answers to Trivia & Facts start on page 111.

32. Who did Sitting Bull meet with after crossing the Canadian border?

33. When asked at this meeting in Canada why he had come, how did Sitting Bull respond?

34. Who were the first people to go back to the Custer Battlefield after June of 1876?

Chief American Horse and family (1891).
Photo courtesy of Little Bighorn Battlefield National Monument.

Answers to Trivia & Facts start on page 111.

35. Pvt. Edward Davern was riding with Lt. Hare toward the ford when he observed across the river, " . . . a few Indians riding their ponies around in circles." What did this mean?

☆   *FACT*   ☆

Custer's was not the worst defeat of United States soldiers in the history of Indian warfare. General Arthur St. Clair on November 4, 1791 had roughly nine-hundred of his men killed by Little Turtle and his coalition in the old Northwest (Ohio Country). Little Turtle was defeated in 1794 at the Battle of Fallen Timbers by "Mad Anthony" Wayne, the chief that never sleeps, (Native American Biography).

36. In 1880 one Indian rode back to the United States, stopping at Fort Buford, to see what kind of reception would be awaiting Sitting Bull's followers if they returned. Who was this friend of Sitting Bull?

37. When Sitting Bull returned from Canada in 1881 how many followers did he have?

☆   *FACT*   ☆

By government estimates, 270,000 Indians in 125 groups dwelled in the country in 1866. Of these, 100,000 could oppose the army and white settlers. (Custer's Controversial Life, p. 250.)

38. Who was the daughter of Chief Little Rock?

39. How was it rumored that the Indians could stop the railroad in 1873?

40. Did Custer learn sign language from the Indians?

Answers to Trivia & Facts start on page 111.

7TH CAVALRY

1. What is the birth date of the 7th Cavalry?

2. What date did Custer join the 7th Cavalry?

3. What was Custer's rank prior to his appointment as lt. colonel?

4. What orders did Custer give at the Battle of the Washita regarding women and children?

5. Captain Louis M. Hamilton was killed at the Washita. Who was his grandfather?

6. In March of 1872 George Custer wrote a letter endorsing someone for 2nd lieutenant in the 7th Cavalry, but he was denied. Whom was he endorsing?

7. How many miles were traveled on the Yellowstone Expedition in 1873?

8. The 7th regimental flag did not fall into Indian hands as did many other guidons. Why not?

9. What were the measurements of Custer's personal headquarters flag?

☆ FACT ☆

Dennis Lynch was the first five year enlistment in the 7th Cavalry. Previous enlistments had been for three years. Lynch was left behind on the steamer Far West *in charge of Custer's baggage,* (Men With Custer).

10. Lt. Donald McIntosh was killed by Indians during the retreat from the Valley, June 25, 1876. What happened to his father when Donald was only fourteen years old?

11. Lt. Hare married whose niece?

Answers to Trivia & Facts start on page 111.

John Burkman (c. 1877).
Photo courtesy of Little Bighorn Battlefield National Monument.

☆   FACT   ☆

Private Archabald Mellhargy and Sergeant Michael
Caddle were good friends. Arch asked Mike to take care
of his family in the event of his death. On June 25, 1876,
he died with Custer. On Christmas Day, 1877, Josephine
Mellhargy and Michael Caddle were married, (ibid).

12. Lt. Nowlan was an academy graduate, but not West Point. Which academy?

13. Who deserted the marines, September 28, 1873 and enlisted in the army the next day?

Answers to Trivia & Facts start on page 111.

☆   *FACT*   ☆

A quartermaster clerk, by the name of Clifton, deserted, leaving behind his wife, who married James Nash in in 1873. She later became the wife of Corporal John Noonan. She died October 30, 1878 and it turned out, "she" was a he. She or he left about $10,000 to the Catholic Church. Corporal Noonan shot himself at Fort Lincoln, November 30, 1878, (ibid).

14. Who was awarded the Medal of Honor but did not receive it?

15. Which 7th Cavalry member also was a sailor and a marine?

16. What did the following members of the 7th Cavalry have in common? Pvt. Pasavan Williamson, Pvt. Joseph Bates, Pvt. John Burkman, Sergeant Hugo Findeisen, Pvt. George Loyd, Corporal John Noonan, Pvt. Robert Rowland, Pvt. Philipp Spinner, Farrier John Stienker and Chief Packer John Wagoner.

17. Pvts. John Day, James Pym, Elijah Strode and James Weeks had what in common?

18. Medal of Honor winner Private Abram Brant did the wrong thing at Camp Ruhlen, Dakota Territory, on October 4, 1878. What did he do wrong?

19. What did Pvts. Charles A. Campbell and Charles W. Campbell have in common beside their name?

20. What did the following members of the 7th Cavalry have in common? Pvts. James Alberts, Nathan Brown, Richard Corwine, David Dewsey, Otto Durselew, Gustave Korn Max Milke, Henry Raichel, William Randall, Francis Roth, William Whitlow, Sgt. Michael Martin, Sgt. George McDermott, Lt. George Wallace and Capt. Owen Hale.

21. Who was shot and killed while trying to escape from the guard house at Ft. Lincoln, April 13, 1877?

Answers to Trivia & Facts start on page 111.

22. Corporal Albert Meyer, Private August Meyer and Private William Meyer were all killed June 25, 1876. Saddler John Meyers made it through without a scratch, lucky guy! What ever became of him?

23. On the first and second of June 1876, the Dakota Column was detained in camp. What held them up?

24. What member of the 7th Cavalry claimed that an Indian was shooting arrows at him from a shotgun?

25. Who had a .45 caliber, 15 pound Sharps telescope rifle made for him in Bismarck?

26. Custer divided his regiment into four battalions June 25, 1876. Which officers commanded them?

27. Shortly after Captain Weir started to move toward Custer on his own, Lt. Hare arrived with an instruction from Reno. What was he instructing Weir to do?

28. When leaving Weir Point, who said the Indians were within 15 feet, firing at him?

29. Private Anton Seibelder, did something unusual for Lt. Varnum on the morning of June 26, 1876. What?

30. While Reno was watering the horses in the Little Big Horn River, where was Lt. Hare?

31. Reno said that Hare, on his own responsibility, using Reno's name, ordered troops to fall back from Weir Point. Is this true or false?

32. Before he died on June 25, Julius Helnier begged something of his comrades. What did he beg for?

33. Who said at the Little Big Horn, "If not careful there would be a second Phil Kearny affair"?

34. What happened when Private Richard Dorn was waking Captain McDougall?

35. Whose picture did Keogh have with him at the time of his death?

Answers to Trivia & Facts start on page 111.

36. An officer held a carbine at a 45 degree angle and fired at a group of Indians thought to be around the body of Lt. McIntosh. The shot fired from Reno Hill scattered the Indians. Who was the officer?

37. John Martin told Benteen the Indians were "skidaddling." True or false?

38. Which trooper was insane with thirst and had to be tied down on the 26th of June?

39. The water carriers brought back water for the wounded. How long did their round trip take?

40. Who was put guard over the water?

41. From Weir Point, Captain Weir saw guidons flying and said: "That's Custer over there." He mounted up ready to go. What changed his mind?

42. Who said, "I thought my situation most desperate and wondered if, after all, the best thing I could do would be to shoot myself"?

43. Which trooper marked his property with the number 50?

44. Which member of the 7th Cavalry served under Custer during the Civil War under the alias of Burns?

45. Whom did the Ree Scouts call "pointed face?"

46. Who said, "I made up my mind that all but one shot would be fired at the Indians and that one would go into my own head, for I had determined never to be taken alive"?

47. Sergeant Charles White gave something to each wounded man on Reno Hill to help ease their suffering. What did he give to them?

48. At the Washita, who decided that if Elliot had not escaped to the wagon train, he must have perished?

49. "It is my opinion that no council can be held with them (Indians) in the presence of a large military force." Who said these words?

Answers to Trivia & Facts start on page 111.

50. What 7th Cavalry officer became a teacher after he was forced to retire due to a wound he received in 1873?

51. Who served as commander of the 7th until the arrival of Colonel Andrew Jackson Smith?

52. Who, in 1867, was the youngest captain, not only in the 7th, but in the entire regular army?

☆   *FACT*   ☆

The 7th Cavalry was a veteran regiment in 1876. Only 10% were new recruits. 75% had one or more years service. Of that 75%, 27% had put in at least one five-year hitch. Twelve men had served fifteen years or more, four had twenty years and one had twenty-five years.

☆   *FACT*   ☆

The actions of his two subordinates left Custer to fend for himself. Reno's retreat from the valley freed all the Indians to concentrate on Custer and Benteen's dawdle brought him to Reno Hill, thus under Reno's command, (ibid p. 188).

53. Captain Barnitz died of complications from a bullet wound he received at the Washita in 1868. How long did he live?

54. Who was known as the "Adonis" of the 7th?

55. What was the "Wild I?"

56. What was Keogh's favorite book?

57. What was the last tune Custer ever heard the regimental band play?

58. What wound did private Nugent receive?

59. How did Custer refer to the Washita Battle?

60. Knipe and Martin were the last men sent back by Custer, but they were not the last to leave and survive. Who was?

Answers to Trivia & Facts start on page 111.

61. While en route with a message from Custer, Sergeant Knipe readied his weapon quickly. Why?

62. Delos G. Sandbertson spent the next six months after the Washita Battle in a hospital. What happened to him?

63. When Custer called a brief meeting the evening of the 24th to inform his officers of a night march, one officer did not attend. Who was the officer?

64. Who said: "I sought death and tried to fight the battle alone"?

65. Custer gave an instruction through his brother Tom to give to Sergeant Knipe. What was it?

66. In the Valley Fight, who was calling the men's attention to his own marksmanship?

67. What were the last words Sergeant Knipe heard Custer say?

68. At what time did Reno reach the top of the bluff after his "charge" from the valley?

69. Captain French said, "I acknowledge that I hate him. That thing knows no more about the Custer fight than any washer woman in Chicago. He was not in it. Before the first shot was fired he was in the bushes and stayed there." Who was it that made French's blood boil?

70. Which member of the 7th Cavalry was called "Bible Thumper?"

71. Regarding alcohol, Custer was a total abstainer, ever since the early stages of the Civil War. There was one recorded incident, however, when he had a touch. What was the occasion?

72. Who had the nickname "Jack of Clubs?"

73. Who claimed to have killed twenty-two Indians at the Little Big Horn?

74. What was Captain French's assessment of Major Reno's performance at the Little Big Horn?

75. How did Elliott attain the rank of major?

Answers to Trivia & Facts start on page 111.

76. In October of 1875 he was stationed at Fort McKavett, Texas with the 10th, one of the army's black regiments. Had she known the fate that lay in store for her son, Mrs. Johnson would have been more than happy to have her son remain with a black regiment. Whose mother intervened on behalf of her son?

77. At Slim Buttes, what guidon did Anson Mills recover?

78. On the Yellowstone Expedition Custer had a *.52* caliber half-stock Springfield rifle. Who, beside Custer, was allowed to use it?

79. Who said, "During the hardest portion of the fight, Reno was hid. I could not find anyone who did see him"?

80. Who was the first trooper killed June 25, 1876?

AFTERMATH

1. In 1878 Lieutenant J. W. Pope visited the Custer Battlefield as a member of General Nelson Miles staff. Sioux scouts, now employed by the army, told him that nearly all Indian casualties occurred where?

2. In what year was an iron fence placed around the monument on Last Stand Hill?

3. Lt. Varnum was not allowed to see any of the Custer dead. Why not?

4. How was Lt. Calhoun identified?

5. On June 29 the last body on Custer Battlefield was buried. Who was it and who buried him?

6. Who buried Boston Custer?

7. When Sgt. Knipe cut open a buffalo robe from around a dead Indian, what did he find?

8. Who said at the Reno Court of Inquiry, "It was not desired that I should tell everything I knew"?

Answers to Trivia & Facts start on page 111.

9. Who wrote Custer's name on a piece of paper and placed it in an expended cartridge shell for future identification of Custer's grave?

10. Who said that he found a note in Cooke's hand that said "Whoever finds this note, give it to Captain Nolan"? The note read, "Capt. Nolan, you may have everything belonging to me."

11. Only two civilians were with the expedition to recover the remains of officers in 1877. Who were they?

12. Who organized the 10th anniversary trip to the Custer Battlefield?

13. What were recruits who joined the 7th Cavalry after June of 1876 known as?

14. Sgt. Joseph McCurry and Pvt. Charles H. Bishop were wounded at the Little Big Horn and Pvt. William Davis was killed. Why did this bother Capt. Benteen?

15. After the Custer Battle, who was in possession of Terry's letter of instruction to Custer?

16. The enlisted men's petition contained how many signatures?

17. Who is thought to have drafted the petition that would attempt to promote Reno and Benteen?

18. What occurred in Lead, South Dakota, on March 11, 1950?

19. Who wrote, "The more I see of movements here, the more admiration I have for Custer and I am satisfied his like will not be found very soon again"?

20. Where and when was the Reno Court of Inquiry?

21. Who was Reno's counsel at the Court of Inquiry?

22. Years after the Battle of the Little Big Horn ex-private Roman Rutten wrote to ex-sergeant Ryan, saying, "I have a grand one." A grand what?

Answers to Trivia & Facts start on page 111.

Nelson A,. Miles.
Photo courtesy of Little Bighorn Battlefield National Monument.

23. What occurred September 9, 1967 that would have disgusted Elizabeth Custer?

24. The mayor of Atlanta, the governor of Georgia and the vice president of Coca-Cola did what together on June 25, 1898?

Answers to Trivia & Facts start on page 111.

☆   *FACT*   ☆

Custer Battlefield National Cemetery was established in 1879 and includes soldiers from abandoned military posts of Montana, North Dakota and Wyoming as well as veterans of the Spanish American War, World War I, World War II, Korean Conflict and Vietnam Conflict, (Custer Battlefield Tour Pamphlet.)

25. Who was the last participant of the Battle of the Little Big Horn to die?

☆   *FACT*   ☆

In Reno's official report, written July 5, 1876, he stated: "We had heard firing in that direction and knew it could only be Custer." At the Court of Inquiry on February 8, 1879, Reno said: "I heard no firing, till after we moved down river some distance." (Little Big Horn Diary, p. 368 and Reno Court of Inquiry).

26. The 7th Cavalry was ordered to the Custer Battlefield to partake in ceremonies for the 50th anniversary. Where was the 7th stationed in 1926?

27. Who wrote the inscription for the marker on Reno Hill Defense Site?

28. On Nelson Miles' visit to Custer Battlefield in June of 1878, who was the female along on the trip?

29. Who suggested to the secretary of war that a suitable monument be erected at the site of Custer's Battlefield?

30. Who wrote, "Bolder movements are generally successful and the general who plans for the enemy and is counseled by his fears, is sure to fail"?

31. After a fire August 16, 1983 at Custer Battlefield, who suggested an immediate archaeological investigation?

Answers to Trivia & Facts start on page 111.

32. Who funded the archaeological survey at Custer Battlefield?

33. Who erected a wooden pyramid on Custer Hill in 1879?

34. When was the present monument on Custer Hill erected?

35. When were the stone markers placed on the Battlefield?

36. In 1926 the National Custer Memorial Association was formed. Who was named as its head?

37. On the 50th anniversary of the battle General Godfrey led the mounted 7th Cavalry to the memorial shaft. Who led the contingent of Indians?

☆ FACT ☆

In June of 1878, Nelson Miles walked his horse over the ground from Reno's last position to the extreme right of Custer's line and it took 56 minutes by his watch. In half the time, Reno could have been in action and at a smart trot or gallop, he could have been on the Indians rear in 15 or 20 minutes - so Miles implied. (ibid p. 245).

☆ FACT ☆

Custer Battlefield entered the national park system as a coordinated area under the general supervision of Yellowstone National Park. Fiscal affairs were under jurisdiction of Yellowstone N.P. until March 1954, at which time Custer Battlefield accounting was taken over by the region two office in Omaha. In March of 1946 the president signed Public Law 332 of the 79th Congress, Second Session, which officially designated the Custer Battlefield a national monument. (ibid p. 90).

38. Who was commanding officer of the 7th Cavalry at the 50th anniversary of the battle?

39. In 1924, whom did General Charles King, U.S. Army, retired, favor as superintendent of Custer Battlefield?

Answers to Trivia & Facts start on page 111.

Crow Scouts, circa 1913. Photo courtesy of Dennis Farioli.

Answers to Trivia & Facts start on page 111.

40. Who was the last veteran Indian Wars superintendent at Custer Battlefield?

☆   FACT   ☆

Since it began functioning in 1953, the Custer Battlefield Historical & Museum Association has purchased many valuable items for donation to the Battlefield Museum collection. These items include the Fred Dustin collection and articles of army and Indian use such as uniforms, equipment and firearms. In 1964 the association purchased a private collection of letters, written to pioneer photographer D. F. Barry by such notables as E. B. Custer, F. W. Benteen and John Martin. The association also commissioned J.K. Ralston to undertake a major painting, Call of the Bugle. *Without the contributions of the CBHMA, the museum would have little significance.* (ibid).

41. What did a storekeeper, a school teacher and an army veterinarian find in 1928?

42. Who was the first man to photograph Custer Battlefield?

43. Lt. Crittenden remained buried where he fell in 1876 for fifty-five years. He was re-buried September 11, 1931 with full military honors, in the national cemetery. Why was he moved?

Answers to Trivia & Facts start on page 111.

LIBBIE

Elizabeth Bacon Custer, 1887. Photo courtesy of Vincent Heier.

1. Speaking of Libbie Custer, who said "We loved him, but we adore her"?

2. The monument to Custer in Monroe, Michigan was sculpted by Edward Potter. What is the name of the monument?

3. On what date was the Monroe statue of Custer dedicated?

4. One sad note crept into Libbie's plans for the dedication of the statue in Monroe. What troubled her?

Answers to Trivia & Facts start on page 111.

5. What were the contents of a July 28, 1877 letter from Major Tilford to Libbie Custer?

6. Elizabeth Custer regretted the loss of something after a fire destroyed their home at Fort Lincoln. What was her regretted loss?

7. Libbie received a telegram on December 9, 1876 that shocked her. What did the telegram say?

8. Who was Doctor Orlen and why did Libbie write to him?

9. After Custer's death, what possible job in Monroe did Libbie consider?

10. Libbie received an unsigned letter late in 1876 informing her of what?

11. What advice did Fred Whittaker give to Libbie?

12. Who said, "Custer's luck was the result of judgment to do the right thing at the right time"?

13. Why did the Detroit Board of Education send a notice to Libbie in April of 1920?

14. For what reason did Libbie not attend the 50th anniversary of the Battle of the Little Big Horn?

15. Libbie wrote to Mr. J.A. Shoemaker of Billings, Montana, and concluded by saying, "In writing this, I feel almost, my husband's hand taking the pen away from me." What disturbed her so, to write this man?

16. Who was Libbie's godson?

17. Libbie Custer and others befriended a young surgeon temporarily stationed at Fort Lincoln in 1875. Who was the doctor?

18. Libbie Custer said of Emanuel Custer, after his death, that he had two dominant passions. What were they?

19. When Richmond fell, Libbie was invited by the Committee on the Conduct of War to visit the city. Where did she stay?

Answers to Trivia & Facts start on page 111.

20. In 1910 Libbie received a letter from a man seeking information about his father. Whom did he claim was his father?

21. General Custer wanted to adopt a ten-year-old boy. Libbie did not. Who was the boy?

22. When Libbie left Fort Lincoln for the last time, the post children came to say good-bye. What did she give to each one of them?

23. What was Libbie referring to when she said, "_____ _____ as much a cavalry charge as any he ever took in the field"?

24. To whom did Custer give orders to kill Libbie if she were in danger of being captured by Indians?

BITS & PIECES

1. At the Battle of the Washita the assistant surgeon in charge, Captain Henry Lippincott, suffered from what problem?

2. How many rounds could a Gatling gun fire per minute?

3. Why did the *Minneapolis Tribune* and the *St. Paul Pioneer Press* publish an interview with D. H. Ridgely on September 8, 1876?

4. What northwestern town was originally called the Crossing?

5. The question of gold in the Black Hills was not considered settled by Custer's 1874 expedition. What happened next?

6. In 1876 the territory of the United States was divided into three military divisions. What were they?

7. The Division of the Missouri had five departments. What were they and who commanded them?

8. Who said, "A Sioux warrior on foot is a Sioux warrior no longer"?

9. Who said, "The Sioux is a cavalry soldier from the time he has intelligence to ride a horse or fire a gun"?

Answers to Trivia & Facts start on page 111.

10. When Custer declined the use of Lowe's Gatling guns, what was Lowe's response?

11. When firing began at Wounded Knee, what startled Varnum?

12. Who told Sgt. John Martin, "Well you are a lucky man and I wish you good fortune"?

13. In what year did English adventurer, Sir George Gore, cross the divide?

14. Years after her husband's death Margaret Calhoun was able to recover something he carried June 25, 1876. What was the item?

15. Who ordered the destruction of a Cheyenne village, June 19, 1867?

16. "This act (the destruction of the Cheyenne village in 1867) brought on another Indian War." Whose opinion was this?

17. Where are Boston Custer and Autie Reed buried?

18. Whom did John Maugham, a New York contractor, marry?

19. The Mary Adam's affidavit was signed January 16, 1878. Who witnessed the signing?

20. Who wrote a booklet *Me and the Black Hills?*

21. Who resigned from the army in 1881 and later became president of the American Woodworking Company?

22. Who was known to the Indians as Bad Hand?

23. Custer's extended leave in New York City was cut short May 18, 1866. For what reason?

24. Who was the white woman found dead after the Battle of the Washita?

25. In late 1875 Custer was offered $200 a night, five nights a week, for four to five months, to do what?

26. "Some think I came here to fight Indians, but I came here to fight Mormons." Whose words were these?

Answers to Trivia & Facts start on page 111.

27. Reno's son married a whiskey heiress, Ittie Kinney, but Reno did not attend the wedding. Why not?

28. Who referred to Sitting Bull as an "inveterate beggar?"

29. Who taught Custer the art of taxidermy?

30. On the Yellowstone Expedition, General Stanley grew to hate something Custer brought along. What was the item?

31. What was the primary task of the infantry with the Dakota Column in 1876?

32. Pvts. William Evans, Ben Stewart and James Bell did what together?

33. Who said, "Inflict soap and a spelling book on every Indian that ravages the plains and let them die"?

34. Can you name the surgeon who was with the Grand Duke Alexis in 1872?

☆   FACT   ☆

John M. Bozeman and John M. Jacobs blazed the Bozeman Trail during the winter of 1862 - 1863, (Custer Cavalry and Crows, p. 51).

35. When did General Custer's last surviving brother, Nevin Custer, die?

36. Alfred Terry spoke two languages besides English. What were they?

37. Why did the Indians call Terry "no hips?"

38. Why did General Terry take a 425 mile stagecoach ride through Montana and Idaho in 1877?

39. What forced General Terry to retire early?

40. In 1951 what ceremony took place far from Custer Battlefield that involved Superintendent Luce?

Answers to Trivia & Facts start on page 111.

41. Custer paid the tuition for a young lady at a private school. Who was this young lady?

42. Supposedly, Custer told Captain Ludlow that, "He had gotten away from Stanley and would be able to swing clear of Terry." Did Captain Ludlow report this?

43. Why was Daniel Brewster riding with Custer in March of 1869?

44. A landmark event in the history of Yankton was the Blizzard of 1873. For years after, how did the townsfolk refer to this storm?

45. How much was it estimated Secretary of War Belknap collected from the Post Tradership Scandal?

☆   *FACT*   ☆

The Anheuser Busch lithograph, Custer's Last Fight, *was first issued in 1896. There were 15,000 copies that year. Since then there have been eighteen subsequent editions, totaling over 1,000,000 copies,* (Greasy Grass Vol. 3)

46. To whom was Tom Custer engaged?

47. Who did Emma Reed, daughter of David and Lydia Reed, marry?

48. According to the Crow scout, Curley, what did Mitch Boyer tell Custer regarding the warriors while they viewed the village from Weir Point?

49. For fifty years after his re-burial in Auburn, New York fresh flowers were left on Keogh's grave three times a year. March 25 (Keogh's birthday), May 30 (Memorial Day) and June 25 (The anniversary of the battle). Who left the flowers?

50. When did "Custer's Luck" desert him?

Answers to Trivia & Facts start on page 111.

51. Identify the seven people in the photo above. *Photo courtesy of Little Bighorn Battlefield National Monument.*

✫ *FACT* ✫

THE POET SCOUT, JACK CRAWFORD

Calling himself the Poet-Scout, a plainsman named Jack Crawford won great fame in the late 1870s by writing poetic verses about the West. Despite spending many years of his adult life in the company of hard drinking dispatch riders and scouts, Crawford never touched liquor, having promised his dying mother that he would not. Flamboyant buckskins, silken ties and long hair made up his appearance, yet his manner was simple and easy. A union soldier at the age of fifteen, Crawford was wounded twice during the Civil War. While recovering from his first wound, a sister of charity taught him to read and write at the age of seventeen. Crawford went on to write four books, three plays and more than 100 short stories. As an army scout and messenger during the Sioux War of 1876, he was held in high esteem by his commanders after several daring rides through hundreds of miles of hostile territory. Crawford's abstinence from liquor was legendary. He once carried a gift bottle of liquor from a friend to Buffalo Bill Cody, which prompted Cody (a celebrated drinker) to say: "I don't believe there is another scout in

*the West that would have brought a full bottle of
whiskey 300 miles." Wild Bill Hickok was moved by the
recital of his poem, "Mother's Prayers." Hickok said:
"You strike a tender spot, old boy, when you talk
mother that way." It was Crawford who would write
Wild Bill's eulogy for him.*

Under the sod in the land of gold, we have laid the fearless Bill;
We called him Wild, yet a little child could bend his iron will.
With generous heart he freely gave, to the poorly clad, unshod;
Think of it pards, of his noble traits, while you cover him with sod.

*A colorful character on the frontier at that time, he
was known to many as Captain Jack and was a close
friend of Buffalo Bill Cody. On July 7th, when the Fifth
Cavalry learned of Custer's death, Cody sent a telegram
to Crawford, then in Omaha, "Jack have you heard of
the death of our brave Custer?" Crawford sent this
reply:*

The Death of Custer

Did I hear the news from Custer? Well I reckon I did old pard;
It came like a streak of lightnin, and you bet it hit me hard.
I ain't no hand to blubber, and the briny ain't run for years;
But chalk me down for a lubber, if I didn't shed regular tears.

What for? Now ye look here Bill, you're a bully boy that's true;
As good as e'er wore buckskin, or fought with the boys in blue.
But I'll bet my bottom dollar, ye had no trouble to muster;
a tear or perhaps a hundred, when you heard of the death of Custer.

He always thought well of you pard, and had it been heaven's will;
In a few more days you'd have met him, and he'd welcome his old
  scout Bill.
For if you remember at Hat Creek, I met with ye General Carr;
We talked of the brave young Custer, and recounted his deeds of
  war.

But little we knew even then pard, and that's just two weeks ago;
How little we dreamed of disaster, or that he had met his foe.
That the fearless reckless hero, so loved by the whole frontier;
Had died on the field of battle, in this our centennial year.

Poet Scout Jack Crawford.
Photo courtesy of Little Bighorn National Monument.

I served with him in the army, in the darkest days of the war;
and I reckon ye know of his record, for he was our guiding star.
And the boys who gathered round him, to charge in the early morn;
Just like the brave who perished, with him on the Little Horn.

And where is the satisfaction, and how are we going to get square?
By giving the Reds more rifles? Invite them to take more hair?
We want no scouts no trappers, nor men who know the frontier;
Phil, old boy you're mistaken, you must have the volunteer.

They talk about peace with these demons, by feeding and clothing
   them well;
I'd as soon think an angel from heaven, would reign with
   contentment in hell.
And some day these quakers will answer, before the judge of us
   all;
For the death of the daring young Custer, and the boys who around
   him did fall.

Perhaps I am judging them harshly, but I mean what I'm telling ye
   pard;
I'm letting them down mighty easy, perhaps they may think it is
   hard.
But I tell ye the day is approaching, the boys are beginning to
   muster,
That the day of great retribution, the day of revenge for our Custer.

And I will be with you friend Cody, my mite will go in with the
   boys;
I shared all their hardships last Winter, I shared all their sorrows
   and joys.
So tell them I am coming friend William, I trust I will meet you ere
   long;
Regards to the boys in the mountains, yours truly in friendship still
   strong.

Crawford later traveled to Fort Fetterman to join Crook's
expedition as a scout.

ANSWERS TO FACTS & TRIVIA

EARLY YEARS ANSWERS

1. Emanuel Custer's first wife. They had three children: Brice W., born 1831; John A., born 1833; and Hannah, born 1830. Hannah lived only one year. Matilda died July 18, 1835 (*Custer: The Controversial Life of George Armstrong Custer*, p. 16).

2. Maria Ward's (Custer's mother). first husband. They were married in 1823 and they had two children, David, born 1824 and Lydia Ann, born 1825. Israel died in 1835 (ibid., p. 17).

3. He was the first surviving child. A son, James, died a few months after birth and in 1838 another son, Samuel, died in infancy. Emanuel's son John also died in 1836 at age 3 (ibid., p 17).

4. Emanuel Custer's younger brother (ibid., p. 18).

5. He was a furniture maker in Cadiz, Ohio, to whom Custer was apprenticed, but the apprenticeship failed (ibid., p. 20).

6. At one time she had entertained the idea that Autie might become a minister (ibid., p.. 25).

7. Beech Point School (ibid., p.. 92).

8. Present day Monroe, Michigan, named for President James Monroe (*Encarta '98*).

9. By chopping wood for the school stove (*Custer the Life of General G.A.C.*, p. 9).

10. Sara McFarland, one of Autie's students (ibid., p. 9).

11. Paul Kuster, a farmer and mason, who left the village of Crefeld in 1684, with his wife Gertrude and four children. They settled at Germantown, Pennsylvania (*Son of the Morning Star*, p. 352).

WEST POINT ANSWERS

1. 1802 (*Custer: The Controversial Life of George Armstrong Custer,* p. 26).

2. His illness was diagnosed as gonorrhea (ibid., p. 34).

3. Artillery tactics. His worst? Cavalry tactics (ibid., p. 39).

4. Patrick H. O'Rorke (ibid., p. 38).

5. Immortals. Goat did not appear until the late 1880s (*Speaking about Custer,* p. 78).

6. West Point friend, Tully McCrea (ibid., p. 23).

7. While not serious in nature, there were 453 offenses (*Custer Legends,* p. 75).

8. 835 (ibid., p. 75).

9. President Lincoln wanted competent officers to train raw troops, due to the outbreak of the Civil War (ibid., p. 75).

10. June 24, 1861 (ibid., p. 75).

11. Colonel John F. Reynolds (ibid., p.76).

12. Peter M. Tyerson and William Ludlow (ibid., p. 76).

13 "Neglect of Duty" and "Conduct to the Prejudice of Good Order and Military Discipline" (ibid., p. 76).

14. "Thro Trials to Triumph" (ibid., p. 92).

15. Phillip H. Sheridan (*Little Bighorn Campaign,* p. 48).

16. Commandant of Cadets. Custer was endorsed by Colonel Sturgis, but the appointment was awarded to Lt. Colonel Emory Upton (*Custer: The Controversial Life of George Armstrong Custer,* p. 289).

CIVIL WAR ANSWERS

1. Brevet Major General Galusha Pennypacker, born June 1, 1844. He was too young to vote until war's end (*Strange and Fascinating Facts*, p. 64).

2 He was an attorney (*Custer Legends, p. 47*).

3. George W. Yates (*Speaking of Custer*, p. 7).

4. May 24, 1862. during a skirmish at the Chichahominy River (ibid., p. 9).

5. Lucretia Beaumont Irwin (Lily). They were divorced January 1867. On February 12, 1872 Yates married Annie Gibson Roberts (ibid., p. 9).

6. Hugh Judson Kilpatrick (*Home At Rest*, p. 29).

7. Elon J. Farnsworth and Wesley Merritt (*Cavalier in Buckskin*, p. 21).

8. "Yankee Doodle" (ibid., p. 24).

9. The use of profanity (ibid., p. 26).

10. Major General Philip H. Sheridan (ibid., p. 27).

11. The Third Division saw action at Tom's Brook Oct. 9, 1864 under Custer (ibid., p. 29).

12. Thomas L. Rosser, Custer's old West Point friend (ibid., p. 29).

13. The Woodstock Races (ibid., p. 29).

14. Each trooper presented a captured battle flag (ibid., p. 30).

15. Secretary of War Edwin M. Stanton (ibid., p. 30).

16. First at Namozine Church and three days later at Sayler's Creek. For his efforts he was awarded two Congressional Medals of Honor (*Cavalier in Buckskin*, p. 32).

17. Frederick Benteen's father, for being a disloyal Southerner (*Son of the Morning Star* p. 31).

18. He was a balloonist employed by the Union to spy on Confederates near Richmond and Custer went with him (ibid., p. 109).

19. He wore a Santa Claus suit (ibid., p. 123).

20. Stephen D. Ramseur. He had just learned of the birth of his daughter the day before he was wounded (ibid., p. 677).

21. Thomas L. Rosser for service in the Shenandoah Valley (ibid., p. 710).

22. Alfred Terry (*Sad and Terrible Blunder*, p. 82).

23. Phil Sheridan (*Touched by Fire*, p. 34).

24. A lieutenant's uniform, a sword, a pistol and spurs at Horstmanns. He then posed for a photograph for his sister (*Custer: The Controversial Life of George Armstrong Custer*, p. 40).

25. Eliza Denison Brown. A runaway slave from a Virginia plantation. She became "the Ginnel's cook." (ibid., p. 107).

26. He was going home to Monroe, to marry Libbie Bacon. The wedding took place on Tuesday, February 9, 1864 at the First Presbyterian Church (ibid., p. 134).

27. Major Jacob Greene, Custer's best-man and young Johnnie Cisco, who held the general's extra horses during battle (ibid., p. 165).

28. Sims states General Lee requested a suspension of hostilities. Custer offered his compliments to General Lee. but to halt his attack he needed an unconditional surrender. Custer sent Chief of Staff Edward Whitaker back with Sims to await a response (*Custer: The Controversial Life of George Armstrong Custer*, p. 224).

29. William Tecumseh Sherman. When the bank failed in 1857, he briefly tried his hand at law, losing the only case he brought to court and then became superintendent of a military academy in Pineville, Louisiana. He said "I can make Georgia howl" and did, with his march to the sea (*Heroes of the Civil War* p. 99).

30. Lee was convinced that Petersburg and Richmond could no longer be held. Lee wanted to move south and link up with General J. E. Johnson's forces who were retreating from General Sherman in North Carolina (*The Civil War Dictionary*, p. 22).

31. Artillery projectile consisting of a tin can filled with cast iron or lead bails set in dry saw dust which scattered immediately on leaving the muzzle. Effective range was 100—200 yards with a maximum range of 400 yards. Its use was primarily defensive (ibid., p. 119).

32. "Army of the Confederate States of America." It was the regular force established by the Confederate Provisional Congress by the act of March 6, 1861. The regular army never existed. The true Confederate Army was the Volunteer or Provisional Army, established in the acts of Feb. 28 and March 6 (ibid., p.169).

33. Obligations of approximately $2,000,000,000 by the end of the war, incurred by the C.S.A, were declared invalid by the 14th Amendment. These were loans from individual states as well as French and English bankers (ibid., p. 179).

34. Died of wounds, also used for administrative abbreviations were M.I.A. for missing in action and P.O.W. for prisoner of war (ibid., p. 132).

35. Shot that was made red-hot for the purpose of setting fire to buildings. It was used during the Confederate bombardment of Fort Sumter (ibid., p. 411).

36. Marcus Albert Reno. Reno was transferred to New Orleans and appointed judge advocate in October, 1865. He was assigned provost marshall in December, 1865 and served in that capacity until August, 1866 (*In Custer's Shadow*, pp. 79-80).

Jacob Greene. Photo courtesy of Little Bighorn Battlefield National Monument.

BLUE COATS ANSWERS

1. In Missouri, Jefferson Barracks for cavalry; David's Island, New York and Columbus Barracks in Ohio for infantry (*Forty Miles a Day* p. *53*).

2. Ten to twelve. Rarely were all units stationed at the same post (ibid., p. *75*).

3. Alcohol. One soldier in every twenty-five was hospitalized as an alcoholic (ibid., p. 159).

4. 140 pounds. 240 pounds with saddle, weapons and equipment (*Bugles, Banners and War Bonnets,* p. 14).

5. A kepi. This is a French word from German origin describing a military hat (ibid., p. 13).

6. Twenty-three years old, thirty-two for a second time enlistee (*Fort A. Lincoln Military Post*).

7. "If the Indians had been confronted by a regiment of magicians and jugglers." (*Son of Morning Star,* p. 2 18).

8. He called it, "The place where the fires of hell had burned out." (*Little Bighorn Diary,* p. 32).

9. Terry did not want to volunteer himself, so he suggested Sykes and Crittenden, but Sheridan rejected them and appointed Terry as the overall commander (*Sad and Terrible Blunder,* p. 17).

10. William Tecumseh Sherman. He was named for the famous Indian leader by his father. After his father's death, he was raised by a local attorney who gave him the first name, William (*Heroes of Civil War,* p. 96).

ARMY SLANG ANSWERS

1. Soldiers carrying a log or saddle as punishment for a minor offense (*Bugles, Banners, War Bonnets,* p. 7).

2. A heavy drinker or drunk (ibid., p. 195).

3. A midday rest for troopers or lunch (ibid., p. 155).

4. Green mules had their tails shaved off so that packers could recognize them. Also, an inexperienced young officer (ibid., p. 195).

5. A horse (ibid., p. 195).

6. To desert, also, French leave (ibid., p. 195).

7. A hot fight or argument (ibid., p. 195).

8. A company of frontiersmen and scouts (ibid., p. . 195).

9. A nickname for being a liar (ibid., p. 195).

10. The choice cut from the upper lip of a mule (ibid., p. 195).

11. A man with a price on his head (ibid., p. 195).

12. Whiskey (ibid., p. 195).

13. Inspected and condemned on a horse (ibid., p. 195).

14. Men addicted to strong drink (ibid., p. 195).

15. A company of men who drank to excess (ibid., p. 195).

16. General Court-Martial (ibid., p. 195).

17. Show cowardice (ibid., p. 195).

18. Hardtack (ibid., p. 195).

19. The top of a man's head or scalp (ibid., p. 195).

20. Coffee (ibid., p. 195).

21. A skulker or loafer; one escaping duties (ibid., p. 196).

22. Tea or anything added to hot water in place of coffee (ibid., p. 196).

23. A striker or servant, extra duty for extra pay (ibid., p. 1996).

24. A buglar (ibid., p.196).

25. A cook (ibid., p. l96).

26. One who enlisted in winter and deserted in spring (ibid., p. 196).

27. An Indian (ibid., p. 196).

28. A bad wetting or heavy rain (ibid., p. 196).

29. Long term service for an officer (ibid., p. 196).

FORTS ANSWERS

1. Because it was found to be very near the geographical center of the United States (*Bugles, Banners and War Bonnets*, p. 15).

2. Fort McKeen (ibid., p. 82).

3. To protect railroad crews from Indians (*National Geographic Map*, December 1986).

4. Fort Shaw. Named for Robert Gould Shaw, it was established as Camp Reynolds in 1867 (*Old Forts NW*).

5. Brevet Major General Philippe Dems de Keredern de Trobriand (ibid., p. 26).

6. Fort Washakie. He was buried with full military honors of a captain (*Native American Biography*).

7. Fort Meade in present day South Dakota was first named Camp Ruhlen (Fort A. Lincoln Military Post).

8. Moses Embree Milner (California Joe) was shot in the back and killed by Thomas Newcomb, the post butcher (*Son Of the Morning Star*, p. 191).

9. Four days later he was turned loose. He became a hunting guide near Gardner, Montana (ibid., p. 192).

10. First known as the Tongue River Cantonment, it was built and commanded by Nelson Miles (*Old Forts*).

11. Fort Assiniboine (Indian for Mountain Sioux). built just 38 miles from the Canadian border, was the largest post ever constructed in Montana (ibid.).

12. Fort Dodge. He was horrified at the quantity of liquor consumed by the officers (*Touched by Fire*, p. 78).

13. *Wa-Cee-Chee,* bad fighter's tepees (*Custer: The Controversial Life of George Armstrong Custer*, p. 251).

14. K.O.W. The literal abbreviation would never do (Fort Lincoln Military Post).

15. Fort Rice, Dakota Territory, June 17, 1873. He wanted to see the Yellowstone Expedition off and meet Custer personally (*Sad and Terrible Blunder*, p. 14).

16. In the summer of 1873 150 carpenters and mechanics under the supervision of General George B. Dandy built Fort Lincoln (*My Life on the Plains*).

CRITTERS & SUCH ANSWERS

1. Byron and Turk (*Bugles, Banners and War Bonnets,* p. 3).

2. Blucher (ibid., p. 57*)*.

3. Walk, 3 & 3/4 mph; trot, 7 & 1/2 mph; and gallop, 10 mph (ibid., p. 199).

4. Because Lt. Varnum said Baker wasn't even present at the Little Bighorn (*Men with Custer*).

5 They stabbed the pony to death. Apparently they didn't have a coin to flip (*March of Montana Column,* p. 95).

6. Hare's horse had been shot through the jaws (Custer In '76, p. 66).

7. About twenty minutes (ibid., p. 66).

8. 26,000 rounds on 13 mules, 2 boxes each, 1,000 rounds per box (ibid., p. 68).

9. To keep the mules off the trail as they were raising too much dust (ibid., p. 78).

10. Boston Custer (ibid., p. 101).

11. He stuffed grass in the horse's mouth (ibid., p, 108).

12. Help shoot about twenty wounded horses (ibid., p, 116).

13. He went down past Moylan's line and east toward the hill. Shots from the Indians cut the ground all around him and Sergeant Hanley thought he would be killed. Hanley felt responsible for him and thought he might be blamed if the Indians got him. Hanley drew his revolver, intending to shoot him before the Indians did, but was able to head him off and ran him back to the herd. "Old Barnum" was a mule (ibid., p. 127).

14. Horseshoes, one front and one rear (ibid., p. 135).

15. A dead trooper (ibid., p. 226).

16. He was riding a mule and he was having trouble keeping up with the rest (ibid., p., 231).

17. Only two (*Keep the Last Bullet for Yourself,* p. 182).

118. James Butler, "Wild Bill," Hickok (*Encarta* 98).

19. He sent them to the Central Park Zoo (*Cavalier in Buckskin,* p. 138).

20. A pet field mouse (*Son of the Morning Star,* p. 205).

21. Dr. C. A. Stein (*Little Bighorn Diary,* p. 32).

22. Captain Keogh and his Irish curses filled the darkness (ibid., p., 244).

23. Custer's horse, Dandy. After recovering from a wound received near Reno Hill, he was sent to Monroe, MI and arrived December 29, 1876 (*Gen. Custer's Libbie,* p. 237).

24. In a letter from his sister, she told Terry that after giving the dog a bath, she counted seventy fleas (*Sad and Terrible Blunder,* p. 275).

25. Buffalo herds (*The Little Bighorn Campaign,* p. 294).

26. He used her to kill his first buffalo. "Lucretia Borgia" was Buffalo Bill Cody's special buffalo gun (*Touched by Fire,* p. 209).

27. Wellington. Ironically, it was a horse he had ridden while at the academy (*Custer: The Controversial Life of George Armstrong Custer,* p. 42).

28. Captain Yates. His future wife, Annie Gibson Roberts, rode fearlessly amid a herd of thundering buffalo and killed two, to the surprise of everyone (*Greasy Grass,* Vol. 8).

29. Tom Custer. While in this condition, he called on all the officers and stayed long enough so they would suspect each other (*Greasy Grass,* Vol., 9).

30. To this day the Arikara people say that the buckskin horse found its way home, a distance of 500 miles, to the village near present day Garrison, N.D (*Greasy Grass,* Vol. 13).

31. It was purchased from Sioux Indians, who had fought Custer and fled to Canada. Major Walsh, of the Northwest Mounted Police, kept the gray for many years as his personal mount and named the horse Custer. (*His Very Silence Speaks,* p. 29).

32. It was a white Indian pony he had found after the Battle of the Little Bighorn (ibid., p. 35).

33. For one of the 41 horses the government paid $90. It was Comanch" and Myles Keogh paid the army the same price. Comanche died November 6, 1891 (ibid., p. 109).

34. Comanche, Montana (ibid.).

35. Dapple Dave, a gray from Company C., 2nd Cavalry, wounded by both bullet and arrow, was the only living thing found after the fight (ibid., p. 319).

36. General Sheridan's horse, Winchester. Sheridan rode him in almost every engagement from 1862 until the close of the Civil War. Winchester died in 1878 (ibid., p. 320).

37. They were all horses belonging to U. S. Grant, during the Civil War. Grant also owned another called Jack, which was his first horse. His favorite was Cincinnati, standing 17 & 1/2 hands high and was rarely ridden by anyone other than Grant himself (one noted exception was Abe Lincoln on his last visit to City Point). During actions around Donelson and Shiloh, Grant rode the roan, Fox, and his mount during the Vicksburg campaign was the ugly raw-boned horse, Kangaroo, left on the field by the Confederates at Shiloh. The black pony named Jeff Davis was captured on the plantation of the brother of the Confederate president, Jeff Davis (*Civil War Dictionary*, p. 353).

38. Bluegrass and Frogtown. Custer later complained, with a chuckle, that he lost $10,000 on them, which he needed for payments on his brother Nevin's farm (*Custer: The Controversial Life of General George Armstrong Custer*, p. 338).

POLITICS ANSWERS

1. Jefferson Kidder, father of Lyman Kidder (*Find Custer,* p. 78).

2. William Belknap (*Custer Legends,* p. 180).

3. That he would not run for a third term (*Encarta* 98).

4. German Chancellor Prince Otto Von Bismarck (ibid.).

5. Fifty-four-thousand, three times that of prewar (*Cavalier in Buckskin*, p. 40).

6. William B. Hazen (ibid., p.125).

7. He was an undercover reporter for the *New York Herald*, sent to investigate post traderships (ibid., p.125).

8. Lt. Harrington (*Son of the Morning Star,* p. 312).

9. He hadn't the slightest military background (*Little Bighorn Diary,* p. 51).

10. It was hoped that the United States Post Office Department, might be induced to issue a special Custer stamp in honor of the 50th anniversary of the general's death (*History of the Custer Battlefield,* p. 79).

11. Defeated presidential candidate Tilden (*Touched by Fire,* p. 10).

12. The Dawes Act. Ironically, Curley's family had an allotment in the valley below Last Stand Hill (*Greasy Grass,* Vol. 4).

RIVERS & BOATS ANSWERS

1. Major William Smith, later paymaster general (*Arikara Narrative*, p. 60).

2. The remains of a cavalry soldier, who had been the victim of torture (ibid., p. *75).*

3. Captain Stephen Baker, 6th Infantry (*The Custer Adventure,* p. 99).

4. A hospital for the wounded (ibid., p. 99).

5. 18" of fresh cut grass, covered with tarpaulins (ibid., p. 99).

6. Doctor Williams (ibid., p. 99).

7. Doctor Porter (ibid., p. 100).

8. David Campbell and John Johnson (ibid., p. 101).

9. Over 20 miles per hour, 1000 miles in 54 hours (ibid., p. 102).

10. John Smith (*Custer In '76*, p.135).

11. Holy Water, Forked River, Elk River, Ash River and Rosebud or Tomato River (ibid., p. 182).

12. Major Orlando H. Moore, 6th Infantry (ibid., p. 190).

13. *The Fletcher* (ibid., p. 227).

14 He was the barber (ibid., p. 240).

15. She hit a cottonwood tree and split her bow. The pumps ran because she was taking on water (ibid., p. 240).

16. A bonfire for 4th of July celebration, They gave up the idea when they heard the bad news (ibid., p. 241).

17. Bighorn, Tongue and Rosebud Rivers (*Encarta 98*).

18. The *Key West* and the *Josephine* (*Cavalier in Buckskin*, p. 119).

19. *The General Sherman* (*Son of the Morning Star*, p. 221).

20. Green wire goggles (ibid., p. 221).

21. They could not walk up a staircase (ibid., p. 222).

22. A prairie fire developed (*Little Bighorn Diary*, p. 6).

23. Lt. Maguires bridging crew (ibid., p. 91).

24. The Powder River. It was also called the filthiest stream in America (ibid., p. 99).

25. Sergeant Henry Fox was about to retire with twenty years service. He was in charge of mail and his unsteady *Machinaw* capsized in the high waters of the Yellowstone. His companions survived, along with the mail, but Sergeant Fox was lost (ibid., p. 128).

26. Captain Mart Coulson (*March of the Columns* p. 45).

27. The daughter of General David Stanley (ibid., p. 191).

SCOUTS ANSWERS

1. Rain, nor sleet, nor dark of night, nor bullets, nor arrows kept "Lonesome Charlie Reynolds" from delivering the mail (*Bugles, Banners and War Bonnets,* p. 94).

2. They sold game meat to the soldiers (*Arikara Narrative,* p. 67).

3 Three: Bloody Knife, Bob Tail Bull and Little Brave (*Greasy Grass,* Vol. 13).

4. Hunkpapa, Eagle Robe Woman (*Hokahey a Good Day to Die,* p. 55).

5. He was hanged for murder (*Custer In 76,* p. 124).

6. Young Hawk (ibid., p. 192).

7. Charles White (ibid., p. 225).

8. Fred Gerard (ibid., p. 228).

9. Fred Gerard (ibid., p. 233).

10. Hairy Moccasin (*Native American Biography*).

11. Scout Ben Clark (*Custer Legends,* p. 63).

12. Medicine Bill Comstock and his Delawares (ibid., p. 82).

13. Buffalo Bill Cody (*Encarta 98*).

14. Buffalo Bill Cody. It was revoked because he was not a member of the military at the time it was awarded (ibid.).

15. Little Beaver (*Cavalier in Buckskin,* p. 65).

16. Scout Ben Clark (ibid., p. 67).

17. She Owl (*Son of the Morning Star,* p. 18).

18. Bloody Knife's wages, $91.66 (ibid., p. 18).

19. Nobody did, but a handyman at Fort Rice, Isaac McNutt, tried (ibid., p. 27).

20. Young Hawk. He preferred death to humiliation, but Sioux bullets missed (ibid., p.28).

21. As punishment for discharging his firearm at a snake, after orders had been given not to do so, as gunfire might alert the hostiles (*Little Bighorn Diary*, p. 69).

22. Reynolds, who normally did not drink, was anxious to get a drink out of Gerard's flask (ibid., p. 282).

23. His cane. The cane was not delivered, however and Hunton had it in his possession until 1921, when he gave it to the Wyoming Historical Society, where it may be viewed today (*March of the Columns*, p. 118).

24. Captain Jack Crawford. He would write his letters in the format of poetry (ibid., p. 116).

25. Lt. Bradley (out of his own pocket). for special services, as his personal travel tutor. Leforge called himself a "White Crow Indian" (*Sad and Terrible Blunder*, p. 113).

26. Wolf or Wolfing was scouting. He was known to the Crows as "Horse Rider" (ibid., p. 114).

27. While chasing antelope, he fell off his horse and broke his collarbone. He could no longer mount or ride a horse (ibid., p. 116).

28. Shows-His-Face, because he resembled a Pennsylvania statesman (ibid., p. 120).

29. Mitch Boyer (*Custer's Last Campaign*, p. 396).

30. Mitch Boyer (ibid., p. 396).

31. So strong was the belief in Custer's invincibility, the three scouts were sent back to General Terry, under guard. If their story was proved to be untrue, they were to be shot as deserters (*Touched by Fire*, p. 340).

32. Dora. She died in young adulthood (*Greasy Grass*, Vol. 4).

33. Curley's grandson was George Old Elk, named for the general himself (ibid.).

MONTANA COLUMN ANSWERS

1. Sergeant M. H. Wilson, 7th U.S. Infantry (*Hokahey a Good Day to Die*, p. 96).

2. First Lt. James H. Bradley (*March of the Montana Column*, p. 172).

3. The body of a dead horse (ibid., p. 172).

4. Barney Bravo (ibid., p. 153).

5. Little Face (*Custer in 76*, p. 168).

6. They got killed by Indians (ibid., p. 251).

7. Privates: Stoker, Raymier and Quin (ibid., p. 25 1).

8. Captain Benham (*Custer on the Little Bighorn*, p. 10).

9. Lt. James H. Bradley (*Custer Legends*, p. 199).

10. Henry Bostwick and Muggins Taylor were each offered $200 to carry out this mission. Both returned (*Custer Cavalry and Crows*, p. 67).

11. Doctor Holmes Paulding (*Sad and Terrible Blunder*, p. 120).

12. It was clear that he was critical of him. He referred to him as "God" and "Old Poppycock." When Major Brisbin and Colonel Gibbon were together, he referred to them as the "Two Generals" (ibid., p. 120).

WYOMING COLUMN ANSWERS

1. George Crook (*Cavalier in Buckskin*, p. 157).

2. Reno was still about 55 miles from the Rosebud Battle, at least two days ride. No chance (*Little Bighorn Diary*, p. 173).

3. "Hit them again and hit them harder!" (ibid., p. 235).

4. An arrow wound to the right hip. Crook recovered, but he carried the arrow point in his hip for the remainder of his life (*Battle of the Rosebud*, p. 12).

5. Red Cloud said this to George Crook, while the latter was trying to recruit Sioux scouts. Not one Sioux joined Crook (ibid., p. 25).

6. Lieutenant Colonel William B. Royal (ibid., p. 26).

7. Major Alexander Chambers, Crook's West Point classmate (ibid., p. 26).

8. John F. Finerty, of the *Chicago Times*, one of several newspaper men along with Crook (ibid., p. 27).

9. At noon on May 29,1876 (ibid., p. 28).

10. To locate Crow and Shoshone scouts (ibid., p. 29).

11. The arrival of the Crow and Shoshone scouts (ibid., p. 44).

12. 176 Crow and 86 Shoshone (ibid., p. 46).

13. Cavalry, infantry, scouts, packers, and miners (ibid., p. 46).

14. General Patrick E. Conner (ibid., p. 47).

15. "The battle where the girl saved her brother." On foot and alone, a Cheyenne warrior by the name of Comes-In-Sight was rescued from certain death by his sister, Buffalo-Calf-Robe-Woman (ibid., p. 60).

16. The scouts wore red strips of cloth tied to their arms. Later they bitterly complained that the soldiers had been shooting at them (ibid., p. 60).

17. Ten soldiers were killed and 23 hostile Indians lost their lives (ibid., p. 87).

18. Captain Guy V. Henry (ibid.).

CHEYENNE & SIOUX ANSWERS

1. The Little Chetish (*Arikara Narrative*, p. 87).

2. He said, It was the first time, he had ever seen a man throw his life away, (*Hokahey,* p. 68).

3. Low Dog (*The Custer Adventure,* p. 78).

4. He took so long to invoke the spirits and consult the medicine man (*Custer In '76,* p. 21).

5. Little Wolf had left the agency with 1000 Northern Cheyenne (ibid., p.212).

6. An individual serving as a tribal policeman (*Keep the Last Bullet for Yourself,* p. 59).

7. Generally considered at age 37 (ibid., p. 57).

8. Nine (ibid., p. 58).

9. An instructor or advisor (ibid., p. 58).

10. American Horse Elder (*Native American Biography).*

11. Gall (ibid.).

12. Together they killed Sitting Bull at Standing Rock Agency, December 15, 1890 (ibid.).

13. Crazy Horse (ibid.).

Major General Guy Vernon Henry was awarded the Congressional Medal of Honor for gallantry at Cold Harbor, Virginia during the Civil War. Portrait in Cullum Hall at West Point. Photo courtesy of Little Bighorn Battlefield National Monument.

14. Witnesses agree Crazy Horse was bayoneted by an enlisted soldier outside the guardhouse at Camp Robinson, Nebraska on the evening of September 5, 1877. In 1903, a former sergeant of the 14th Infantry identified Pvt. William Gentles as the man who killed Crazy Horse and most writers have accepted it as fact. However three other individuals specifically refute that Gentles was responsible (*Greasy. Grass,* Vol. 12).

15. He assassinated Spotted Tail (*Native American Biography*).

16. Gall (ibid.).

17. Iron Tail (ibid.). V

18. Slow (ibid.).

19. Kicking Bear (ibid.).

20. In 1932 White Bull told Vestal that he killed Custer (ibid.).

21. The honorary killer of Custer (*Custer on the Little Bighorn*, p. 23).

22. The murders of Balliran and Honsinger in 1873. The judge dismissed the case (ibid., p. 27).

23 Wear a war bonnet, having earned the right by participating in combat with male warriors (ibid., p. 37).

24. In the region of Grand River about 1831 (*Encarta 98*).

25. Wovoka, a Piaute prophet, also called Jack Wilson (1856-1932). (ibid.).

26. "Allies" (ibid.).

27. Santee, Nakota and Teton (ibid.).

28. The Ojibwa (ibid.).

29. One Stab. The others were frightened away, but One Stab remained as a guide for Custer (*Cavalier in Buckskin*, p. 137).

30. His six year-old son, instructing him to give it to the major (*Son of the Morning Star*, p. 220).

31. His autograph. Today it is worth upwards to ten thousand dollars (ibid., p. 230).

32. J. M. Walsh of the Canadian Mounted Police (ibid., p. 302).

33. He said: "We are British Indians. Our grandfathers were raised on British soil," (ibid., p 302).

34. Wooden Leg and nine other Cheyenne (ibid., p. 342).

35. It indicated that an enemy had been sighted and warned to prepare for trouble (*Little Bighorn Diary*, p. 272).

36. One Bull (ibid.).

37. 187 (*Sad and Terrible Blunder*, p.272).

38. Mo-nah-se-tah, "Young Grass that Shoots in the Spring." Her father was killed at the Washita (ibid.,, p. 287).

39. If they could kill Big General Rosser (*Custer 7th Cavalry and the Campaign of 1873*, p. 27).

40. No. While stationed in Texas in 1865, Custer learned sign language from children in an asylum for deaf and dumb (*Greasy Grass*, Vol. 11).

7TH CAVALRY ANSWERS

1. July 28, 1866 (*Bugles, Banners and War Bonnets*, p. 1).

2. November 3, 1866 at Fort Riley (ibid., p. 2).

3. Captain in the regular army (ibid., p. 3).

4. Avoid killing any but fighting men (ibid., p. 56).

5. Alexander Hamilton (ibid., p. 53).

6. Brother Boston Custer (ibid., p. 76).

7. 935 miles (ibid., p. 85).

8. The flag was carried by the regiment to the Little Bighorn, but was encased and placed with the pack train (ibid., p. 125).

9. 36" high, 5 1/2' long, center of swallow tail cut back 22" (ibid.).

10. His father was also killed by Indians (ibid.).

11. General Winfield Scott Hancock (ibid.).

12. The Royal Military Academy. He served for a time in the British army (ibid.).

13. Oscar Pardee did and was assigned to Company L, 7th Cavalry. He should have stayed in the marines because he died with Custer (ibid.).

14. Private Niel Bancroft was awarded the Medal of Honor, October 5, 1878, but did not receive it because he was discharged on September 20, 1878 and could not be located. He died not knowing he had been awarded the nation's highest honor (ibid.).

15. Private James Barsantee, Company B, was a sailor in the U.S. Navy from 1867-1869. He also served as a private in the U.S. Marine Corp. He deserted March 29, 1877 at Fort Lincoln and was never apprehended (ibid.).

16. Suicide (ibid.).

17. They were all murdered (ibid.).

18. While handing his revolver to the first sergeant, he accidentally shot and killed himself (ibid.).

19. They both died on the same day, August 2, 1906 (ibid.).

20. All were killed in battles with Indians after the Little Bighorn (ibid.).

21. Private John McShane (ibid.).

22. He died of a wound from the Tongue River Battle in 1877 (ibid.).

23. A heavy snow storm (*Arikara Narrative*, p. 67).

24. Private Edward Pigford (*Hokahey a Good Day to Die*, p. 93).

25. Sergeant Ryan (*Hokahey A Good Day to Die*, p. 94).

26. Benteen, Reno, Keogh and Yates (*Custer in 76*, p. 54).

27. Open up communications with Custer (ibid., p. 56).

28. Lt. Edgerly (ibid., p. 57).

29. Varnum was so worn out Seibelder carried him sound asleep, down to the hospital and covered him up (ibid., p. 67).

30. He went down the valley one mile with the scouts (ibid., p. 65).

31. False. Hare says Reno was mistaken. Says he did no such thing (ibid., p. 67).

32. He begged for them to put him out of his misery (ibid., p. 67).

33. Captain McDougall (ibid., p. 71).

34. Dorn was shot and killed (ibid., p. 71).

35. McDougall's sister (ibid., p. 72).

36. Lt. Godfrey (ibid., p. 76).

37. False, of this he was positive (ibid., p. 101).

38. Private Cornelius Cowley (ibid.).

39. 1 and 1/2 hours (ibid., p. 115).

40. Lt. Varnum (ibid., p. 115).

41. Sergeant Flanagan pointed out that what he saw wasn't Custer, it was Indians (ibid., p. 129).

42. Henry Petring (ibid., p. 134).

43. Nathan Short (ibid., p. 137).

44. Dennis Lynch (ibid., p. 138).

45. Lt. Varnum (ibid., p. 185).

46. Peter Thompson (*Keep the Last Bullet for Yourself*, p. 179).

47. He had a glassful of jelly and he gave each one a spoonful (*They Rode with Custer*).

48. Captain Myers, in charge of one search party (*Custer Legends*, p. 63).

49. Lt. Colonel George A. Custer (ibid., p. 79).

50. Lt. Charles Braden (*Home at Rest*, p. 11).

51. Major John W. Davidson of the 2nd Cavalry (*Cavalier in Buckskin* p. 44).

52. Louis M. Hamilton. He was 22 years old (ibid., p. 46).

53. Forty-four years. He died in 1912, from a growth around his wound (*Son of the Morning Star*, p. 186).

54. Lt. James Calhoun (ibid., p. 263).

55. Keogh's I Company (ibid., p. 291).

56. *Charles O Malley, The Irish Dragoon* (ibid., p. 292).

57. "Garry Owen," (ibid., p. 294).

58. A bullet hit a canteen cork, which flew up and hit him between the eyes, while he was attempting to get water for the wounded (ibid., p. 321).

59. He called it "A regular Saylor's Creek," (*Cavalier in Buckskin*, p. 75).

60. Peter Thompson (*Custer in 76*, p. 125).

61. He was startled by a group of Indians, which turned out to be Ree Scouts (ibid., p. 93).

62. He had been scalped, but lived to tell about it! (*Son of the Morning Star*, p. 164).

63. Benteen. He said he did not know where the officers had gone. It would not be the last time he would be absent (*Little Bighorn Diary*, p. 244).

64. Captain French (ibid., p. 311).

65. "Go to Captain McDougall. Tell him to bring the pack train, straight across the country. If the packs come loose, cut them and come on quick - a big Indian camp. If you see Captain Benteen, tell him to come quick - a big Indian camp," (ibid., p. 292).

66. Captain French (ibid., p. 288).

67. "Hold your horses boys, there are plenty of them down there for all of us." Knipe noticed a number of troopers' horses galloping ahead of Custer as the sergeant was departing (ibid., p. 292).

68. According to Lt. Wallace, it was between 3:15 and 3:30 P.M. (ibid., p. 321).

69. Lt. DeRudio (*Captain of Chivaric Courage*, p. 47).

70. Lt. Mathey. He had studied for the priesthood in France, but somehow he became an agnostic and joined the army (*With Custer's Cavalry*, p. 195).

71. The wedding of Lt. Gibson and his new bride, Katherine, to toast the couple (ibid., p. 198). *Editor's Note: As I portray Mrs. David Reed, the oldest step-sister of the general, it is my responsibility to maintain and uphold the abstemious nature of General Custer, for it is Mrs. Reed who insisted that the general make a vow never to partake of liquor. The exact quote from* With Custer's Cavalry *regarding the wedding toast is as follows: "When it came to drinking the health of the bride and groom, every eye glanced surreptitiously at General Custer, wondering what he would do. As the toast was proposed and given, he nodded smilingly, lifted the punch to his lips, wet them slightly, then replaced his glass, practically untouched. However, considering that he was a total abstainer, Frank and I felt that he had paid us a particular honor in swallowing even a few drops" (*With Custer's Cavalry, p. 1986*).

72. Lieutenant Hodgson (*Custer Battle Casualties*, p. 127).

73. Captain French (*Captain of Chivalric Courage*, p. 18).

74. He said he would have been justified in shooting Reno and assuming command in the valley (ibid., p. 18).

75. He took the commissioned officer's test after the Civil War and scored so highly he was elevated to the rank of major (*Touched by Fire*, p, 160).

76. Lt. William Van Wyck Reily (*Greasy Grass*, Vol. 12).

77. Company I's, along with Myles Keogh's gauntlets (*Greasy Grass*, Vol. 4).

78. Because of his unusual talent as a sharpshooter, Private Tuttle was permitted to use it (*Custer's 7th and the Campaign of 1873*, p. 207).

79. Captain French (*Captain of Chivalric Courage*, p. 29).

80. Sergeant O'Hara (*Custer in 76*, p. 118).

AFTERMATH ANSWERS

1. Calhoun Ridge (*Hokahey a Good Day to Die,* p. 61).

2. 1884 (ibid., p. 71).

3. Reno had him posted on high ground, east of Custer Battlefield, to watch for Indians as a punishment for adding to notes Reno tried to send out June 26 (ibid., p. 63).

4. By fillings in his teeth (ibid., p. 63).

5. Lt. Mathey buried civilian reporter, Mark Kellogg (*Custer In 76* p. 79).

6. Lt. Godfrey (ibid., p. 76).

7. Several white scalps (ibid., p. 96).

8. Trumpeter John Martin (ibid., p. 101).

9. Lt. Wallace (ibid., p. 110).

10. While this is very doubtful, John Foley of Troop K said that he found such a note in the lieutenant's hand. Foley, who buried Cooke, also said that he found the head of a trooper under a kettle (ibid., p. 147).

11. John Baronett and George Harendeen (ibid., p. 226).

12. Colonel Herbert J. Slocum. Slocum graduated from the military academy on June 22, 1876 and was transferred to the 7th Cavalry effective July 28 that year. He said they camped on the bottom under the battlefield with tents. Benteen and McDougall and plenty of others got drunk. They camped for a week and had a royal time (ibid., p. *254).*

13. "The Custer Avengers" (ibid., p. 269).

14. They were players on Benteen's baseball team (Fort Lincoln Military Post).

15. Libbie Custer. General Custer sent it to her for safekeeping (*Custer Legends,* p. 193).

16. 235 (ibid., p. 206).

17. First Sergeant Joseph McCurry of Benteen's Company H (ibid., p. 207).

18. Charles Windolph, the last white survivor of the Custer Battle died. He was 98 years old. Buried in the Black Hills National Cemetery, his cause of death was listed as senility (*Men With Custer*).

19. Nelson A. Miles. Custer's exact like may not have been found, but Nelson Miles is as close as it gets (*Cavalier in Buckskin,* p. 204).

20. Chicago's Palmer House, January 13, 1879, lasting almost a month (*Son of the Morning Star*, p. 10).

21. Lyman Gilbert, a civilian (ibid., p. 10).

22. An Anheuser Busch lithograph (ibid., p. 21).

23. Major Reno was re-buried with full military honors at Custer National Cemetery (ibid., p. 48).

24. They were pallbearers for Captain Benteen (ibid., p. 40).

25. Dewey Beard or sometimes called Iron Hail. He died in November of 1955.

26. Fort Bliss, Texas (*General Custer's Libbie*, p. 319).

27. General Godfrey. It was dedicated August 14, 1929 and no names were used (ibid., p. 321).

28. The wife of Colonel Sturgis. For some reason she believed her son, Jack, was still among the living. She finally accepted the reality of her son's death (*Custer Battle Casualties*, p. 66).

29. Quartermaster General Montgomery C. Meigs. He also suggested that the remains of the enlisted men be interred in a common grave at the base of the monument (ibid., p. 69).

30. Thomas L. Rosser. August 16, 1876, letter to Major Reno (*Custer Myth*, p. 231).

31. Park Superintendent James V. Court (*Custer and His Times, Book Three*, p. 149).

32. The Custer Battlefield Historical & Museum Association (ibid., p. 150).

33. Captain George K. Sanderson (*Markers Artifacts and Indian Testimony*, p. 2).

34. In 1881. Lt. Charles F. Roe interred the remains of the enlisted men around the perimeter. In 1884, an iron fence was placed around the monument to prevent vandalism (ibid., p. 2).

35. In 1890 by Captain Owen Sweet. 249 stones were cut, 246 stones were placed. Civilians and scouts were not entitled to the military stones (ibid., p. 5).

36. General Godfrey (*History of the Custer Battlefield*, p. 80).

37. White Bull, a nephew of Sitting Bull and one time hostile (ibid., p. 80).

38. Colonel Fitzhugh Lee (ibid., p. 82).

39. King sought to obtain the appointment of Theodore Goldin. The appointment might have been made had it not been for General Godfrey. Godfrey opposed it on the grounds that he believed Goldin to have intentionally made false statements about the battle (ibid., p. 117).

40. Eugene Wessinger. Because of vandalism in 1915, he suggested that an iron fence be placed around the markers on Last Stand Hill. It wasn't until 1930 that the fence was erected (ibid., p. 117).

41. Joseph A. Blummer, R.G. Cartwright, and Colonel Elwood L. Nye found hundreds of expended *.45/55* carbine cases scattered along what is now called Nye-Cartwright Ridge (*Custer's Last Campaign*, p. 362).

42. John H. Fouch, most likely. On July 5, 1877, Fouch took two photographs: "View down the ravine on Custer Field" and "The place where Custer fell." Of the two, only the latter exists (*Greasy Grass*, Vol. 7).

43. It was said to make way for the road to Reno-Benteen defense site, but the superintendent of the national cemetery said the grave was not receiving proper care. The road had nothing to do with it (*Greasy Grass*, Vol. 11).

LIBBIE ANSWERS

1. General George Spaulding at a dinner before the dedication of a monument to General Custer in Monroe (*Custer Legends*, p. 23).

2. *Sighting the Enemy* (ibid., p. 21).

3. June 4, 1910 and President Taft was there with Libbie at the dedication as well as 25,000 spectators. The statue weighed 7,500 pounds (*General Custer's Libbie*, p. 301).

4. If she could have selected one person to accompany her to the dedication, it would have been the general's sister, Maggie. Maggie had been sick with cancer and died March 22, 1910 (ibid., p. 298).

5. Custer's remains were shipped by U.S. Express to West Point, along with a lock of Custer's hair for Libbie. Major Tilford kept a lock of the general's hair for himself (*Son of the Morning Star*, p. 344).

6. Newspaper articles about Custer and a wig made from Custer's hair (ibid., p. 345).

Sighting the Enemy, *the monument in Monroe, Michigan, sculpted by Edward Potter.*
Photo courtesy of Nora Whitley.

7. Captain Weir had passed away (*General Custer's Libbie*, p. 236).

8. He was Captain Weir's physician and Libbie wrote requesting the details of Weir's death (ibid., p. 236).

9. Postmistress in the Monroe post office (ibid., p. 238).

10. During a séance in Brooklyn, the general had allegedly been contacted and wanted Libbie to know he was happy and for Libbie not to grieve, it was all for the best (ibid., p. 238).

11. Write! Do not be afraid to write of yourself. It is through your memories that Custer's best traits will gradually and unconsciously expand to the world (ibid., p. 240).

12. Nelson Miles in a letter to Libbie, emphasizing Custer's success (ibid., p. 245).

13. A new school would open in September of 1921 on Midland and Linwood Avenues and would be named General George A. Custer School (ibid., p. 310).

14. Her friend, David F. Barry, who had been a photographer at Fort Lincoln and knew the Custers well, advised against it. He thought it would be a great mental strain for her to be shown certain parts of the Battlefield (ibid., p. 317).

15. Mr. Shoemaker started a movement to unveil a monument to Major Reno during the semi-centennial of the battle. In Libbie's letter to Shoemaker she said of Reno words she had kept hidden for fifty years. She referred to Reno as " . . . so great a coward," " . . . so unworthy a man" and " . . . so faithless a soldier" (ibid., p. 3 17).

16. George L. Yates, the son of Captain George and Annie Yates (ibid., p. 321).

17. Lt. Holmes Offley Paulding, later with the Montana Column (*Sad and Terrible Blunder*).

18. Religion and politics. Emanuel Custer died in 1892 (*Touched By Fire*, p. 10).

19. In the mansion of Jefferson Davis (ibid., p. 45).

20. Moses Embre Milner "California Joe," (ibid., p. 150).

21. Custer's namesake, Autie Reed (ibid., p. 190).

22. A small photograph of General Custer (ibid., p.308).

23. Custer's proposal of marriage (*Custer: The Controversial Life of George Armstrong Custer*, p. 129).

24. William W. Cooke (ibid., p. 248).

BITS & PIECES ANSWERS

1. Snow blindness (Bugles, Banners and War Bonnets, p. 56).

2. 250 (ibid., p. 85).

3. Ridgely was a trapper and claimed to have been a prisoner of the Sioux at the time of the Custer Battle. He told reporters that he had witnessed some of the action of the fight. Before the end of September the editors of the *Pioneer Press* received a letter from Mr. T. A. Ward of Anoka, Minn. telling that he knew the whereabouts of Ridgely at the time in question and it wasn't with the Sioux. From this point on, Ridgely is lost to history, (ibid., p. 149).

4. Bismarck, North Dakota (*National Geographic Map*, December 1986).

5. Another expedition, in 1875 was sent out by the Interior Dept. headed by mining engineer, Walter P. Jenny, and escorted by troops under Colonel R. I. Dodge (*Arikara Narrative*, p. 21).

6. The Missouri, the Atlantic and the Pacific (ibid., p. 22).

7. The Department of the Dakotas - Brig. Gen. Alfred Terry.

   The Department of the Platte - Brig. Gen. George Crook.

   The Department of the Missouri - Brig. Gen. John Pope.

   The Department of Texas - Brig. Gen. E. O. C. Ord.

   The Department of the Gulf - Brig. Gen. C.C. Auger (ibid., p. 22).

8. Little Phil Sheridan (ibid., p. 81).

9. George Crook (ibid., p. 81).

10. Lowe wept (*Custer In '76*, p. 53).

11. Varnum had his pipe shot from his mouth (ibid., p. 63).

12. General Alfred Terry (ibid., p. 105).

13. 1856 (ibid., p. 222).

14. His watch (*Cyclorama of Custer's Last Fight*, p. 54).

15. General Winfleld S. Hancock (*Custer Legends*, p. 79).

16. Indian Commissioner N. G. Taylor (ibid., p. 79).

17. Woodland Cemetery in Monroe, Mich. (ibid., p. 92).

18. Years after her husband's death Maggie Calhoun, Custer's sister, married John Maugbam (ibid., p. 93).

19. George P. Flannery, a notary public in Bismarck, witnessed the signing that attested to the fact that General Terry gave Custer permission to use his own judgment. Terry came into Custer's tent

where Mary was present and she heard Terry say, "Custer, I don't know what to say for the last." Custer replied, "Say whatever you want to say." Terry then said, "Use your own judgment and do what you think best if you strike the trail" (ibid., p. 200).

20. Ed Ryan, who claimed he was left behind by Custer in 1874 to care for a sick comrade. Ryan was not interested in facts. However, he was interested in selling his booklet to tourists. The old fraud became the source of much irritation to Major Edward Luce while he was superintendent of the Custer Battlefield National Monument. Luce proved that Ryan's name does not appear in army records in that time period and he also proved that Custer had died ten years before Ryan was born! (ibid., p. 218).

21. Frederick Dent Grant. He returned to the army in 1898 and became a major general in 1906. He died in 1912 and is buried at West Point (*Home at Rest,* p. 27).

22. Ranald Slidell Mackenzie. A number of his fingers were missing from war wounds. He died in 1889 and is buried at West Point (ibid., p. 30).

23. The sudden death of Judge Bacon, Custer's father-in-law (*Cavalier in Buckskin*, p. 39).

24. Mrs. Clara Blinn and her child (ibid., p. 71).

25. The Redpath Lyceum Bureau wanted him to lecture (ibid., p. 154).

26. Frederick Benteen, during a confrontation that led to his court-martial in 1887 (*Son of Morning Star,* p. 34).

27. Reno's new wife, Isabella (married in 1882), did not care for Ross and would not attend. Marcus decided if she refused to go, he also would not attend (*In Custer's Shadow,* p. 337).

28. Buffalo Bill Cody (ibid., p. 2131).

29. Mr. C. W. Bennet, while on the Yellowstone Expedition in 1873 (ibid., p. 232).

30. A stove. Stanley ordered him to get rid of it, so he hid it in Captain French's wagon. Stanley discovered this and had Custer placed under arrest (ibid., p. 235).

31. To protect the supply train and base camp (*Little Bighorn Diary,* p. 6).

32. Carried a letter from Terry to Crook, arriving July 12 (*March of the Columns,* p. 118).

33. Mark Twain (ibid., p. 165).

34. Imperial Surgeon, Doctor Condrin (*Register of Custer Battlefield National Monument Photo Col.*, p. 9).

35. February 25, 1915 (*General Custer's Libbie*, p. 309).

36. French and German (*Sad and Terrible Blunder*, p. 80).

37. Because of his slender build, 6 feet 2 inches and 180 pounds (ibid., p. 80).

38. To meet with Sitting Bull at Fort Walsh, across the Canadian border. Terry would offer him a full pardon in return for guns and horses (ibid., p. 271).

39. He had Bright's disease (inflammation of the kidneys), complicated by gout. He died December 16, 1890 at his home at 30 Hillhouse Street in New Haven, Conn. He is buried at the Grove Street Cemetery (ibid., p. 278).

40. The transfer of the white towel, used as a Confederate surrender flag at Appomattox Court House in 1865. The towel had been part of Elizabeth Custer's estate and was personally carried to Appomattox Court House by Superintendent Luce and presented by Colonel Brice C. W. Custer (*History of the Custer Battlefield*, p. 93).

41. His baby sister, Margaret (*Touched by Fire*, p. 190).

42. No! The source was not Ludlow, but Colonel Robert Hughes, ever-loyal brother-in-law of General Terry (ibid., p. 302).

43. The Cheyenne held his sister, Mrs. Anna Morgan, hostage. Custer negotiated her release and also that of twelve year-old Sarah Catherine White (*Custer Controversial Life*, p. 285).

44. They called it "The Custer Storm of 1873." The Custer's arrived April 10 and the storm followed shortly thereafter (ibid., p. 297).

45. Belknap and his two wives (after his first wife died in 1870, Belknap married her sister), collected an estimated $20,000 (ibid., p. 332).

46. Lulie G. Burgess, of Jersey City, New Jersey. She influenced Tom to re-dedicate his life to Christ. In frail health and after a long illness, she passed away (*Greasy Grass*, Vol. 9).

47. Fred Calhoun, brother of Lt. James Calhoun. They were married February 20, 1879 (*Greasy Grass*, Vol. 10).

48. He thought the warriors were out campaigning somewhere else (*Little Bighorn Diary*, p. 291).

49. In 1927, the flowers stopped coming and eighty-six year old Nellie Martin, who had so faithfully brought the flowers over the years, was buried next to the one she so long loved and honored (*Honor of Arms,* p. 181).

50. Easy answer. On June 25, 1876 "Custer's luck" had deserted him and so had the majority of his command. Over one-half of his regiment had failed to come to his aid when he had summoned them and when he had need them the most. Strange to say, no explanation has been requested of, nor disciplinary action leveled at, the officer whose duty it was to respond to Custer's last order (*Custer Legends,* p. 173).

51. This will remain an open question. Send your identification of people in photo to Dennis Farioli, c/o CBHMA, P.O. Box 902, Hardin, MT 59034-0902.

INTRODUCTION TO TRIVIA IN NOVELS, POETRY, ART, MOVIES AND TV

Vincent A. Heier

Ever since I was seven years old, I have been fascinated by George Armstrong Custer and the Battle of Little Big Horn. After seeing Custer depicted in the old TV western, *Cheyenne,* and staring with wonder at the "barroom" art of Otto Becker's *Custer's Last Fight,* I was hooked. Then my father read me Quentin Reynold's biography *Custer's Last Stand* and Errol Flynn left the lasting portrayal of Custer in the film *They Died With Their Boots On*, and I knew I was forever to be linked with seeking out the "facts" about the Custer story.

The problem was these early images only perpetuated a myth. They were far from factual and unfortunately have fostered further misinformation which is repeated even by professional historians and writers, causing history buffs like me to cringe. And yet the more I discover the facts, the more complicated, and fascinating, the Custer story becomes. Also, these faulty versions have added to the poppularity and endurance of Custer's myth.

Ever since the CBHMA began the annual quiz published in *The Battlefield Dispatch*, I would read over the questions and moan. I thought I knew a lot, but where did they come up with these seemingly impossible questions?

Also, each spring, my good friend and fellow Custer enthusiast in Missouri, Gary Gilbert, would call me to confer on the answers. While two heads are better than one, I must confess that even that left me with a headache. Yet what amazed me then, and now, was how Gary would consistently find the answers and very often would be one of those finalists who made the "Last Stand" in winning the quiz.

That's why, a few years ago, I decided if I couldn't beat them, I would join them. When Dennis Farioli approached me for help in writing the Annual Quiz, I jumped at the chance. To become a co-conspirator in digging up the trivial pursuit of Custer was a challenge I would enjoy. Since my own interest in Custer began from media images and second-rate art and literature, the evolution of the legend behind the facts has been a special fascination for me. Thus I was asked to concentrate some of my questions in these areas. Hence this has been my main contribution to this book of Custer "facts."

And yet while there are many facts - some easily identified and some more obscure - these questions and answers are not offered to "trivialize" the Custer saga. His enduring persona and the mystery of his last battle continue to inspire those who deal in facts, or shape these facts in new and intriguing ways.

So while I may have early-on been misled by the inaccuracies of television, art, movies, and juvenile biographies, I owe their creators - as should we all - a debt of gratitude for helping us want to discover not just the facts, but the enduring meaning. That's why this book is not only a book of trivia, it is a storehouse of history to enable all of us to discover the truth on a subject whose legacy will long endure.

Vincent Heier
St. Louis, MO
May, 1999

TRIVIA IN NOVELS

1. What was the title of the novel authored by the anti-Custer biographer, Frederick Van de Water?

2. Teat is a novel dealing with which famous casualty of the Little Big Horn?

3. Who wrote the 1882 dime novel on Custer?

4. Which book was described by western historian Bernard DeVoto as ". . . a sound history of the Little Big Horn campaign and almost a good novel"?

5. Which novel was based on the fictional journal of Col. John Buell Clayton, a former Confederate who lived with the Indians until the eve of the Little Big Horn?

6. How old is Jack Crabb at the beginning of the novel *Little Big Man*?

7. In Usher Burdick's novelette, *Tragedy in the Great Sioux Camp*, there is an imaginary romance between a Sioux girl and which Seventh Cavalry soldier?

8. What do the juvenile Custer novels, *Last of the Thundering Herd*, by Bigelow Neal; *Buffalo Chief*, by Jane and Paul Annixter; and *Comanche*, by David Appel have in common?

9. *The Silent Eaters* by Hamlin Garland is the fictional biography of which Indian leader at the Little Big Horn?

10. Little Big Horn novel, *Winter Count*, was written by whom?

11. The first fiction accounts of the Little Big Horn appeared in 1876 in what form?

12. What were the names of the two scouts sent by Custer to determine Indian strength before the battle in the novel *Cache La Poudre*?

Answers to trivia questions start on page 163.

13. How does Custer meet his fate in Frederick and Frank Goshe's book *The Dauntless and The Dreamers* (1963)?

14. In Douglas Jones' *The Court-Martial of George Armstrong Custer,* under what condition would Custer resign from the army?

15. Who is described by Jack Crabb in Thomas Berger's novel, *Little Big Man*, as having ". . . had a face full of sharpened edges - he was a living weapon"?

16. What is the title of the Custer novel written by Harry Sinclair Drago?

17. What is unique about Michael Blake's novel, *Marching to Valhalla*?

18. *The Convenient Coward*, by Kenneth Shiflet, is a fictional account about which Seventh Cavalry officer?

19. Which novel was subtitled, *A Romance of Custer and the Great Northwest*?

20. Who wrote the novel?

21. What is the name of the character in a Custer novel who is described as "six feet of whiskered distinction in full evening dress and tails"?

22. What is the name of the hero of *Bugles in the Afternoon*?

23. Name the author who penned the "Son of the Plains" trilogy on Custer.

24. What novel tells the story of Yellow Bird, Custer's Cheyenne son, and his fight to survive in a strange land?

25. Which Custer-related short story was voted as among the best science-fiction stories and depicted the Little Big Horn as an air battle?

26. Which 7th Cavalry officer shared the affections of the heroine Crimson Royale in Paula Fairman's novel, *The Tender and the Savage*?

Answers to trivia questions start on page 163.

27. What two authors wrote Custer-related novels with the same title, *A Good Day to Die?*

28. Give two of the pen names of Henry Wilson Allen.

29. Who wrote the Custer novel *Bugles West?*

30. Name the fort substituting for Ft. Lincoln in the 1956 novel *The Dice of God.*

31. The novel, *Yellow Hair,* deals with which famous battle?

32. Name the main character in Lewis Patten's 1968 novel, *The Red Sabbath.*

33. Name the author of the 1980 Custer novel, *A Mighty Afternoon.*

34. What is the Little Big Horn novel written by Earl Murray?

35. Name the character who serves as prosecutor in *The Court-Martial of George Armstrong Custer.*

36. Which novel, which climaxes at the Little Big Horn, tells the story of a young Indian boy, Tacante, Buffalo Heart?

37. Name three writers who authored biographical novels on Crazy Horse.

38. Which Custer novel has the main character survive the Alamo and end up at Little Big Horn?

39. In which William Safire novel does Custer appear briefly as an aide to General McClellan?

40. Who wrote the Custer 1894 dime novel, *Custer's Last Shot or the Boy Trailer of the Little Horn?*

41. Who wrote the book *Libbie: A Novel of Elizabeth Bacon Custer?*

42. In the romance novel, *Cody's Last Stand,* what is the unique connection between lovers Cody and Elizabeth?

43. Who authored *A Road We Do Not Know: A Novel of Custer at the Little Big Horn?*

Answers to trivia questions start on page 163.

44. Who wrote the 1942 Custer novel, *The Renegade*?

45. Name two Custer novels written by Randall Parrish.

46. Name the time-travel novel where the hero attempts to warn Custer of his impending doom with the help of Mark Twain?

47. Which novel is subtitled *An Epic of the Seventh Cavalry*?

48. In Loring MacKaye's juvenile novel, *The Great Scoop,* the young hero becomes friends with which noted victim of the Little Big Horn?

49. Name the cavalry officer ". . . whose iron will would bend to no man's, not even Custer's" in the novel *Broken Eagle*?

50. Who wrote the alternative history novel, *The Indians Won*?

Henry Wadsworth Longfellow from the Vincent A. Heier Collection

Answers to trivia questions start on page 163.

TRIVIA IN POETRY

1. What are the titles of the two versions of Walt Whitman's Custer poems?

2. Henry Wadsworth Longfellow immortalized which Indian warrior in which epic poem?

3. What is the title of the poem authored by Custer's first biographer, Frederick Whittaker?

4. Who wrote the 1876 poem, *Custer's Immortality*?

5. What is the title of the 1876 poem written by Leavitt Hunt read during the unveiling of the Custer statue in Monroe, Michigan, in 1910?

6. What fellow officer and contemporary of Custer penned a poem entitled *Custer's Last Charge*?

7. Who wrote *Custer and Other Poems*?

8. What are the titles of the sections of John Neihardt's *The Song of The Indian Wars* dealing specifically about Custer?

9. Which famous Montana artist penned a Custer poem?

10. What is the title of John Greenleaf Whittier's poem about the Little Big Horn?

11. In Richard Brautigan's 1968 verse, he compares the Little Big Horn to which other disaster?

12. What is distinctive about John Hay who wrote the 1880 poem *Miles (sic) Keogh's Horse*?

13. Who was the African-American "poet-evangelist" who wrote *Custer's Last Ride* in 1877?

14. What was the title of the popular 1960 song sung by Larry Verne?

15. Who wrote this song?

Answers to trivia questions start on page 163.

16. Johnny Horton, known for his historic ballads of the 1950s, recorded which song about Custer?

17. Which Seventh Cavalry officer wrote a poem on Custer?

18. Which poem of anonymous authorship was picked up in the road near the camp of the 1st Connecticut Cavalry, June 1865?

19. Who wrote the poem, *War With The Sioux (1876)*.

20. For whom was G. A. Davis' 1897 poem, *A Mourner* written?

21. Which poem was written and delivered for the 1910 unveiling of the Custer statue in Monroe, Michigan?

22. Where was Charles B. Davis' poem on Custer published?

23. What is the most frequently reproduced of all Custer ballads?

24. Which composer is known for writing pieces about Napoleon, Gettysburg, and Custer's Last Stand?

25. Which song was composed especially for the 1879 unveiling of Custer's statue at West Point?

26. Who wrote this song?

27. In the album, *Bitter Tears*, who sang "Now I will tell you busters / I'm not a fan of Custer's"?

28. Who composed this song?

29. What was the name of the Navajo rock group who performed the song *Custer's Last Stand?*

30. Besides the song *Garry Owen,* what is the second song mostly associated with the Seventh Cavalry?

31. Which poet penned works on Wounded Knee and Sitting Bull?

32. Which young Canadian Indian wrote *Custer's Day?*

33. Which poem relates the controversy regarding removing the horse Comanche's remains?

34. Who wrote the first poem about the Battle of the Little Big Horn?

Answers to trivia questions start on page 163.

35. Who first compared the Custer battle with the famous *Charge of the Light Brigade?*

36. Poet Thomas Rossman described which 7th Cavalry officer as the *Chief with the Silvery Crown?*

37. Who wrote a poem denouncing attempts to avenge Custer in 1876?

38. For the tenth anniversary of the Little Big Horn, what Indianapolis poet wrote that the nation should " . . . carve high their names on glory's scroll"?

39. What holiday was commemorated by poet Sam T. Clover in his 1894 verse on the battle?

40. Who wrote "In the valley of the Little Big Horn, history explodes into quiet"?

41. Which poem includes the typographical error "Yellow Hare" instead of "Yellow Hair?"

42. Which poet saw the " . . . great Comanche" at Ft. Lincoln and penned the verse *Old Comanche?*

43. Which poem began with the words "Oh Custer - gallant Custer! Man foredoomed"?

44. Where was Audrey Souder Buck's poem, *Custer's Grave* printed?

45. P. W. Norris memorialized which Little Big Horn participant in his 1883 poem?

46. P. N. Norris served in what government position in the West?

47. Which poem fabricates a conspiracy to get rid of Custer?

48. Who wrote the long and critical Custer battle poem, *The Golden Eagle?*

49. What two poems on the Little Big Horn were written by Joaquin Miller?

Answers to trivia questions start on page 163.

50. To whom did George Custer write a short verse?

TRIVIA IN ART

1. Which artist did the first illustration of Custer's Last Stand?

2. Which two famous artists feuded over the painting *Custer's Demand*?

3. Artist Gayle Hoskins' painting, *Custer's Last Fight,* was used on the dust jacket for which classic book?

4. Name the two "last stands" painted by Montana artist James K. Ralston.

5. Who is depicted in Schreyvogel's painting, *Custer's Demand*?

6. What happened to the original Cassilly Adams' painting, *Custer's Last Fight*?

7. Which company popularized the 1896 lithograph *Custer's Last Fight* by Otto Becker?

8. For the 1889 painting, *Custer's Last Stand,* artist William Edgar Paxson consulted which 7th Cavalry officer?

9. Which artistic depiction of the Custer battle is commented upon in Ernest Hemingway's book, *For Whom the Bell Tolls*?

10. Who painted *Custer's Last Stand: A Bar Room Picture in the St. Louis Mode*?

11. What other panels surrounded Cassilly Adams' *Custer's Last Fight* painting?

12. John Mulvaney's *Custer's Last Rally* came into the possession of which famous company?

13. Which disciple of Carrie Nation took an axe to a copy of Otto Becker's lithograph when it was on display in the Kansas State Historical Museum?

14. Which famous battle painting was on display at the Chicago World's Fair in 1893?

Answers to trivia questions start on page 163.

15. Which famous Custer painting is on display at the Karl May Museum in Dresden, Germany?

16. Where was there a 1968 exhibition of Custer's Last Stand art shown?

17. What two national magazines commissioned "last stand" paintings for the 75th anniversary of the battle?

18. What "last stand" painting was described by poet Walt Whitman as " . . . an artistic expression for our land and people"?

19. The Whitney Gallery of Western Art in Cody, Wyoming purchased William E. Paxson's *Custer's Last Stand* for what amount?

20. What company commissioned H. Charles McBarron's *Custer's Last Stand*?

21. What brand of cigarettes featured an ad with an N.C. Wyeth picture of the "last stand?'

22. What magazine featured a Custer's Last Stand cartoon with the caption, "Who said that blondes have more fun?"

23. Who painted the 1876 lithography, *Custer's Last Charge*?

24. What noted artist illustrated the children's book, *The Story of General Custer*?

25. What artist was commissioned by author John S. duMont for his booklet, *Firearms in the Custer Battle*?

26. What artist's "last stand" was used to illustrate Hamlin Garland's 1898 article, "General Custer's Last Fight as Seen By Two Moon?"

27. Rufus Fairchild Zogbaum provided illustrations for which of Mrs. Custer's books?

28. Who painted *The Last Glow of a Passing Nation*?

29. What were the dimensions of Cassilly Adams' *Custer's Last Fight*?

Answers to trivia questions start on page 163.

30. Who gathered Red Horse's pictographs of the Little Big Horn in the *Tenth Annual Report of The Bureau of Ethnology*?

31. What were the dimensions of John Mulvaney's *Custer's Last Rally*?

32. Which Custer battle artist served with the 1874 Northern Boundary Commission escorted by Major Reno?

33. Who illustrated the E. E. McVey pamphlet, *The Crow Scout Who Killed Custer*?

34. Who painted the 18 foot long picture, *After The Battle*?

35. What two other Custer paintings are located in the Karl May Museum in Dresden, Germany?

36. What famous artist grew up considering Custer as one of his "greatest idols?"

37. Who painted *The Rushing Red Lodges Passed Through the Line of the Blue Soldiers*?

38. Who painted the 1967 work, *A Gathering of the Chiefs*?

39. Who was commissioned to provide art for the 1969 edition of the official handbook of Custer Battlefield?

40. Which famous comic strip featured Colonel Fluster of the 4,187th Cavalry?

41. Which image of Custer was deemed too graphic and not included in the first printing of the 1969 *Custer Battlefield Handbook*?

42. Which "last stand" picture was first reproduced in the June 15, 1915 issue of *The Mentor*?

43. What was the full name of artist N. C. Wyeth?

44. Which famous company published chromolithographs of most Civil War battles as well as one entitled *Battle of the Little Big Horn*?

45. Which battle painting depicts Custer astride his horse charging in victory?

Answers to trivia questions start on page 163.

46. Who painted the battle picture, *To The Last Man, June 25, 1876?*

47. Which artist's original oil of the "last stand" is in the West Point museum?

48. Who painted the "last stand" picture which is used on the 1996 brochure of the Little Big Horn Battlefield National Monument?

49. J. Steeple Dairs' 1897 picture called *Custer's Last Fight* was published in what book?

50. Whose battle painting was used on the program of the 75th Anniversary of the Battle of the Little Big Horn?

TRIVIA IN MOVIES & TV

1. Which actor played Captain Myles Keogh in *Tonka* and General Custer in *The Great Sioux Massacre?*

2. Which officer who died with Custer was eulogized by John Wayne (Captain Nathan Brittles) in *She Wore a Yellow Ribbon*?

3. Who played Custer in the short-lived TV series, *The Legend of Custer*?

4. Which character actor played Gen. Sheridan in *They Died With Their Boots On* and as General Howe in *Sitting Bull*?

5. Who played the Cheyenne Indian leader in *Custer of the West*?

6. What was so unusual about the location of the Little Big Horn battle scenes in *Little Big Man*?

7. Who is the actor who played Custer in two films and what are the two films?

8. The title of the film, *They Died With Their Boots On*, originally was taken from a book about whom?

9. Which actor played the Indian captured by Cody and Hickok who described the fate of Custer in the 1939 film, *The Plainsman*?

Answers to Trivia in Movies & TV start on page 170.

10 What was the major chronological flaw regarding Custer's character in the film *Santa Fe Trail?*

11. Who played Custer in the film *Santa Fe Trail?*

12. The character of "Queen's Own Butler" in *They Died With Their Boots On* was loosely based on which Seventh Cavalry officer?

13. The *Glory Guys*, a veiled retelling of the Little Big Horn story, was based on which novel?

14. The 1951 film *Warpath* was based on which Custer related novel by Frank Gruber?

15. Which famous TV dad and character actor played Lieutenant Cooke in the film *Bugles in the Afternoon?*

16. Which director was responsible for the two Custer-related films: *Sitting Bull* and *The Great Sioux Massacre?*

17. Who played Elizabeth Custer in the TV movie, *The Court-Martial of George Armstrong Custer?*

18. Which two actors portrayed Custer in different episodes of the TV western, *Cheyenne?*

19. How did Clint Walker, TV's Cheyenne, survive the Battle of the Little Big Horn?

20. Which film began with the narration: "Custer is dead and around the bloody guidon of the immortal Seventh Cavalry lie the bodies of 212 officers and men"?

21. Who played General Winfield Scott in *They Died With Their Boots On?*

22. What do Chief Thundercloud, Victor Mature, Will Sampson and Michael Greyeyes have in common?

23. What "thirty-something" actor played Custer in the TV movie, *Crazy Horse?*

24. In which John Wayne movie do the characters visit Little Big Horn Battlefield?

Answers to trivia questions start on page 163.

25. The film, *Legends of the Fall,* tells the fictional story of what Custer- related character?

26. The film, *Seventh Cavalry,* was based on what short story?

27. What do character actors Charley Grapewin and Slim Pickens have in common?

28. Where are the names of the three modern national guard soldiers who end up fighting with Custer at the Little Big Horn in TV's *The Twilight Zone*?

29. Which TV comedy used footage from *They Died With Their Boots On* to open the show?

30. According to the TV western, *Branded,* who tutored Autie Custer at West Point?

31. What was the title of *The Twilight Zone* episode referring to Custer?

32. Who was originally slated to direct *They Died With Their Boots On*?

33. Who finally directed the film *They Died With Their Boots On*?

34. Which popular book on the Battle of the Little Big Horn was made into a 1992 movie?

35. What connection does the movie *E.T.* have with *Son of the Morning Star*?

36. Who played Custer in the TV film, *Son of the Morning Star?*

37. Marcello Mastroianni portrayed Custer in which foreign film?

38. In the TV movie, *The Legend of the Golden Gun,* Keir Dullea's Custer parodied which famous general?

39. Sheb Wooley played Custer in which 1951 film?

40. What was the title of the Three Stooges short in which they scouted for Gen. Muster?

41. What movie was directed by and starred Francis Ford as Custer?

Answers to trivia questions start on page 163.

42. Name three films released to coincide with the 50th anniversary of the Little Big Horn?

43. Who starred in the 1951 film, *Little Big Horn*?

44. The Walt Disney film, *Tonka,* was based on what book?

45. What film provoked Charles Reno, grandnephew of Major Reno, to sue its producers?

46. Which actor had been originally signed to portray Custer in the TV movie, *Son of the Morning Star*?

47. Who played Custer in an episode of the TV show *Branded*?

48. Who portrayed Sitting Bull in the film *Buffalo Bill and the Indians or Sitting Bull's History Lesson*?

49. Who played Libbie Custer in the TV movie *Son of the Morning Star*?

50. Where were the last stand scenes filmed in *They Died With Their Boots On*?

51. Who played Custer in a cameo role in *The World Changes*?

52. What is the name of the Indian Mrs. Custer visited to find out what happened to her husband in the Wyatt Earp episode, "The General's Lady?"

53. What was the name of the screenwriter who was denied screenwriting credit for *They Died With Their Boots On*?

54. Which silent film, based loosely on the Custer story, included a last stand where "gambler, priest, general and scout" fall?

55. What was the name of the disgraced soldier who wins redemption at the Little Big Horn, as played by Hoot Gibson in *The Flaming Frontier*?

56. Which Custer movie's writers were criticized by *The New York Times* as being " . . . writers in warbonnets" who scalped history?

57. Which western film includes last stand like references to a grand painting called *Thursday's Charge*?

Answers to trivia questions start on page 163.

58. Who played Custer in John Wayne's *The Searchers*, but was not included in the final film?

59. How many died in the making of *They Died With Their Boots On*?

60. Who played Major Reno in *The Great Sioux Massacre*?

61. Custer's Last Stand in *The Plainsman* looked remarkably like which artist's last stand?

62. Which Little Big Horn epic starred Charlton Heston as Custer?

63. The Little Big Horn was used as a prelude to the action for which film?

64. What do the TV programs *Gunsmoke, Have Gun Will Travel, Yancy Darringer,* and *Time Tunnel* have in common?

65. What was the name of the character who portrayed Custer in the film spoof *Won Ton Ton, the Dog Who Saved Hollywood*?

66. Lincoln Tate played Custer in which film?

67. What was interesting about the casting of Mary Ure as Libbie Custer in *Custer of the West*?

68. Who played Custer in Walt Disney's *Tonka*?

69. In the 1940s which famous character actor was to play a villainous Custer in a never-made film titled *Seventh Cavalry*?

70. How much money was budgeted for the film, *They Died With Their Boots On*?

71. Which 1913 silent film included the Battle of Summit Springs, the death of Sitting Bull, and the tragedy at Wounded Knee?

72. This 1926 silent film, billed as " . . . the supreme achievement in western epics," had Dustin Farnum as Custer?

73. Which Custer film had as a special guest of honor General Edward S. Godfrey at its premiere?

74. Custer was portrayed by whom in the 1916 serial, *Britton of the Seventh*?

Answers to trivia questions start on page 163.

75. In 1936 the 15-episode serial, *Custer's Last Stand,* was released with whom as an elderly-looking Custer?

76. Which character actor appeared in the Custer-related films: *The Massacre; The Plainsman; They Died With Their Boots On; Fort Apache; Sitting Bull; and The Great Sioux Massacre?*

77. Custer's character in the *Glory Guys* was renamed what?

78. Who played Custer in a cameo appearance in the 1966 remake of *The Plainsman?*

79. Who played Custer in the TV film, *The Court-Martial of George Armstrong Custer?*

80. Who portrayed Sitting Bull in two different movies and what were the movies?

81. Rodney A. Grant portrayed whom in *Son of the Morning Star?*

82. What Indian languages were spoken in the film *Son of the Morning Star?*

83. Sitting Bull was played by whom in *Son of the Morning Star?*

84. What were the titles of the two-part TV *Cheyenne* episodes dealing with Little Big Horn?

85. What *Bonanza* star portrayed as army investigator to Major Reno in the *Cheyenne* Custer episode?

86. What gift does Custer give Jason McCord on *Branded?*

87. Who played a villainous Custer in an episode of TV's *Yancy Derringer?*

88. Paul Kelly played Custer in what Wallace Berry - Marjorie Main western of 1940?

89. Who played Custer as a "glory hunting, racist" in the 1954 film, *Sitting Bull?*

90. Who played Major Reno and Captain Benteen in *Custer of the West?*

91. Who portrayed Custer in the TV film, *The Class of 61?*

Answers to trivia questions start on page 163.

92. Who played the scout, Bloody Knife, in the TV film, *Son of the Morning Star*?

93. Who portrayed Custer in the serial, *The Oregon Trail*?

94. In the TV show, *The Life and Legend of Wyatt Earp*, which Seventh Cavalry officer asked for help from Wyatt Earp?

95. Which Custer film depicted the death of Isaiah Dorman?

96. Who played Captain Tom Custer in *The White Buffalo*?

97. Who played Custer in the film *Warpath*?

98. Taylor Nichols and Jason Leland Adams each played Custer in this TV series?

99. Who played Custer in the 1937 non-western film, *The Plainsman*?

100. What Custer movie was billed as "The most thrilling film ever seen, costing more than $30,000.00"?

Post card of 1909 movie Custer Massacre *from the Vincent A. Heier Collection.*

Answers to trivia questions start on page 163.

Henry Wilson Allen used the pens names of Will Henry and Clay Fisher to write many books based on American history. This picture is from the jacket of his novel, Custer's Last Stand. *Courtesy of the Vincent A. Heier Collection.*

Answers to trivia questions start on page 163.

ANSWERS TO TRIVIA IN NOVELS

1. *Thunder Shield* (Dippie, *Custer's Last Stand*, p. 69).

2. Isaiah Dorman (Gould, Theodore Anthony Teat).

3. Frederick Whittaker (*Custer's Last Stand*, p. 66).

4. *Bugles In The Afternoon* (Dippie, *Custer's Last Stand*, p. 70).

5. *No Survivors* (Henry, Will, *No Survivors*).

6. 111 years old (Dippie, *Custer's Last Stand*, p. 73).

7. Lieutenant James Butler (Dippie, *Custer's Last Stand*, p. 74).

8. Story told by animals, (Dippie, *Custer's Last Stand*, p. 74).

9. Sitting Bull (Garland, Hamlin, "The Silent Eaters," in *The Book of the American Indian*, pp. 157-274.)

10. D. Chief Eagle, (Chief Eagle, D., *Winter Count)*

11. Dime novels (Dippie, *Custer's Last Stand*, p. 66).

12. Buckskin Joe and Jerome James (Dippie, *Custer's Last Stand*, p. 80).

13. Suicide (Dippie, *Custer's Last Stand*, p. 74).

14. He would receive the Medal of Honor (Jones, Douglas C., *The Court-Martial of George Armstrong Custer).*

15. Crazy Horse (Berger, *Little Big Man*, p. 415).

16. *Montana Road* (Drago, Harry Sinclair, *Montana Road*).

17. This fiction book is written from Custer's point of view as his own journal (Blake, Michael, *Marching to Valhalla).*

18. Major Marcus Reno (Shiflet, Kenneth E., *The Convenient Coward).*

19. *Britton of the Seventh,* (Brady, Cyrus T., *Britton of the Seventh: A Romance of Custer and the Great Northwest*).

20. Cyrus Townsend Brady (Brady, *Britton of the Seventh).*

21. Flashman in *Flashman and the Redskins* (Fraser, George MacDonald, *Flashman and the Redskins).*

22. Kern Shafter, (Haycox, Ernest, *Bugles in the Afternoon).*

23. Terry C. Johnston: *Long Winter Gone, Seize the Sky, Whisper of the Wolf.*

24. *Whisper of The Wolf* by Terry C. Johnston.

25. "Custer's Last Jump" (Utley, Steven & Waldrop, Howard, "Custer's Last Jump," in Terri Carr's *The Best Science Fiction of the Year #6*, pp. 291-331.)

26. Tom Custer, (Fairman, Paula, *The Tender and the Savage).*

27. Thomas Wakefield Blackburn (*A Good Day to Die,* 1967) and Del Barton (*A Good Day to Die*, 1980).

28. Will Henry and Clay Fisher (Dippie, *Custer's Last Stand,* p. 197).

29. Frank Gruber (*Bugles West*, 1954).

30. Ft. Doniphan (Birney, Hoffman, *The Dice of God*, p. 16).

31. The Battle of the Washita (Fisher, Clay, *Yellow Hair*).

32. Scout Miles Lorette (Patten, Lewis B., *The Red Sabbath*).

33. Charles K. Mills (*A Mighty Afternoon*).

34. *Flaming Sky* (Murray, Earl, *Thunder in the Dawn*).

35. Major Gardiner (Jones, *Court-Martial of,* p. 5).

36. G., Clifton Wisler's *Lakota* (1989).

37. Mari Sandoz (*Crazy Horse: Strange Man of the Oglalla,* 1975); Will Bevins (*Stone Song*, 1995); and Bill Dugan (*Crazy Horse: War Chiefs,* 1992).

38. *The Scream of Eagles,* by William W. Johnstone (1996).

39. *Freedom* (Safire, William, 1987).

40. Col. J. M. Travers (Wide Awake Library, No. 565, 1883).

41. Judy Alter (1994).

42. John Cody is a descendant of Sitting Bull and Elizabeth Lawrence is related to Custer (Clark, Kathy, *Cody's Last Stand*).

43. Frederick J. Chiaventone (1996).

44. L. L. Foreman (*The Renegade,* 1971).

45. *Bob Hampton of Placer* (1906) and *Molly McDonald: A Tale of the Old Frontier* (1912).

46. *Twice Upon a Time* by Allen Appel (1988).

47. Robert Vaughan's *Yesterday's Reveille* (1996).

48. Mark Kellogg (1956).

49. John Singetary (Oliver, Chad, *Broken Eagle*).

50. Martin Cruz Smith (1970).

Dime novels from the Vincent A. Heier Collection

ANSWERS TO TRIVIA IN POETRY

1. *A Death-Sonnet for Custer* and *From Far Dakota's Canons.* (Dippie, Brian & Carroll, John, *Bards of the Little Big Horn*, pp. 22 & 24).

2. *The Revenge of Rain-in-the-Face* (Dippie & Carroll, *Bards*, p. 242).

3. Captain Jack Crawford (Dippie & Carroll, *Bards*, p. 59).

4. Laura S. Webb (Dippie & Carroll, *Bards,* p.62).

5. *The Last Charge* (Dippie & Carroll, *Bards*, p.72).

6. William Ludlow (Dippie & Carroll, *Bards*, p.73).

7. Ella Wheeler Wilcox (Wilcox, Ella Wheeler, *Custer, and Other Poems*, pp. 94-134; Dippie & Carroll, *Bards*, p.100).

8. VIII. The Yellow God; XI, The Seventh Marches; XII High Noon on the Little Horn (Neihardt, John G., *The Song of the Indian Wars*, pp. 139-143; Dippie & Carroll, *Bards*, p.168).

9. J. K. Ralston (Dippie & Carroll, *Bards*, p.168).

10. *On The Big Horn* (Dippie & Carroll, *Bards*, p. 244).

11. The sinking of the *Titanic* (Brautigan, Richard, *The Pill Versus the Springhill Mine Disaster,* p. 3; Dippie & Carroll, p. 234).

12. John Hay was a distinguished statesman who once served as President Lincoln's personal secretary (Dippie & Carroll, *Bards*, p. 234).

13. Albert A. Whitman (Dippie & Carroll, *Bards*, p. 74).

14. *Mr. Custer* (Dippie & Carroll, *Bards*, p. 33).

15. Al Duval, Cal Rogers, and Marc Fredricks (Dippie & Carroll, *Bards*, p. 33).

16. *Comanche (The Brave Horse)* (Dippie & Carroll, *Bards*, p. 33).

17. Albert Barnitz: *With Custer at Appomattox* (Dippie & Carroll, *Bards*, p. 288.).

18. *The Heroes of the Custer Tie* (Dippie & Carroll, *Bards*, p. 287).

19. Maud M. Simmerlee (Simmerlee, Maud M., *United States History in Rhyme*, p. 212; Dippie & Carroll, *Bards*, p. 131).

20. As a tribute to Mrs. Custer (Dippie & Carroll, *Bards* p. 19).

21. *The Heart and the Sword*, by Will Carleton.

22. *The Teepee Book I* (June, 1915, p. 2). (Dippie & Carroll, *Bards* p. 204).

Ella Wheeler Wilcox in 1896. Photo courtesy of Vincent A. Heier.

23. *Custer's Last Charge* (Dippie & Carroll, *Bards* p. 322).

24. E.T. Paull (Dippie & Carroll, *Bards*, p. 316).

25. *Hail and Farewell to Custer!* (Dippie & Carroll, *Bards*, pp. 316-317).

26. Henry Morford (Dippie & Carroll, *Bards*, p. 316).

27. Johnny Cash (Dippie & Carroll, *Bards*, p. 331).

28. Peter LaFarge (Dippie & Carroll, *Bards*, p. 331).

29. Silverbird (Dippie & Carroll, *Bards*, p. 331).

30. *Sergeant Flynn* (Dippie & Carroll, *Bards* p. 329.).

31. James H. McGregor (Dippie & Carroll, *Bards*, p. 261).

32. John LeCaine (Woonkapi-Sni) ("Custer's Day," in Gontran LaViolette's *The Sioux Indians in Canada*, pp. 77-79; Dippie & Carroll, *Bards*, p. 259).

33. Robert E. Haggard's, *Cavalry-On-Wheels* (Amaral, Anthony A., *Comanche: The Horse That Survived the Custer Massacre*, pp. 60-61; cf Dippie & Carroll, Bards, p. 237).

34. J.S. Carvell, July 8, 1876 (Walker, Judson Elliot, *Campaigns of General Custer in the North-West, and the Final Surrender of Sitting Bull*, pp. 120-121; cf Dippie & Carroll, Bards, p. 18).

35. Lt. Edward Maguire (Dippie, Brian, W., *Custer's Last Stand: The Anatomy of an American Myth*, p. 12).

36. Captain Frederick Benteen (Dippie & Carroll, *Bards*, p. 186).

37. Father William J. McClure in *Extermination* (Dippie & Carroll, *Bards*, p. 68).

38. A. P. Kerr in *Custer's Last Charge: June 25, 1886* (Dippie & Carroll, *Bards*, p. 212).

39. Decoration Day (Dippie & Carroll, *Bards* p. 213).

40. William Stafford's, *At the Custer Monument* (Brown, R.D.; Kranidas, Thomas; & Norris, Faith G., editors, *Oregon Signatures*, pp. 84-85; Dippie & Carroll, *Bards*, p.227).

41. *Sunrise on Custer Battle Field*, by Arthur Chapman (*The Teepee Book*, II (June, 1916), p. 13; Dippie & Carroll, *Bards*, p. 224).

42. William V. Wade (Dippie & Carroll, *Bards*, p. 232).

43. *Chivalry's Afterglow*, by Henry Morford in *Algernon Sydney Sullivan*, by Anne Middleton (pp. 146-147; Dippie & Carroll, *Bards*, pp. 211-212).

44. A postcard (Dippie & Carroll, Bards,, p. 230).

45. Charley Reynolds (Norris, P.W., *The Calumet of the Couteau and Other Poetical Legends of the Border*, pp. 60-62; Dippie & Carroll, *Bards*, p. 182).

46. He was second superintendent of Yellowstone National Park (Dippie & Carroll, *Bards*, p. 182).

47. Charles P. Green's *Custer Framed* (1931) (Green, Charles P., *Ballads of the Black Hills*, pp. 123-125; Dippie & Carroll, *Bards*, p. 159).

48. Quentin Waight (*Prelude to Glory*, p. 11-34; Dippie & Carroll, *Bards*, p. 266).

49. *Custer and His Three Hundred* (1876) and *Custer* (1890) (Dippie & Carroll, *Bards*, p.5 4).

50. Mary Holland (Monaghan, Jay, *Custer: The Life of General George Armstrong Custer*, p. 10-11).

ANSWERS TO TRIVIA IN ART

1. William R. Cary (Russell, Don, *Custer's Last*, p. 15).

2. Frederic Remington and Charles Schreyvogel (Dippie, Brian W., *Custer's Last Stand: The Anatomy of an American Myth*, p. 38).

3. *The Custer Myth* by William Graham (Graham, W. A., *The Custer Myth*, 1953).

4. *Custer's Last Hope* and *Call of the Bugle* (Dippie, *Custer's Last Stand*, p. 47).

5. Little Heart, Lone Wolf, Kicking Bird, Satanta, Grover the Scout, George Custer, Thomas Custer, J. Schuyler Crosby, and Philip Sheridan (Hutton, Paul A., editor, *The Custer Reader*, p. 224).

6. It was destroyed June 13, 1946, in a fire at the Fort Bliss, Texas officers' club. (Russell, *Custer's Last*, p. 34).

7. Anheuser-Busch Brewing Co. (Russell, *Custer's Last*, p. 33).

8. Lt. Edward S. Godfrey (Dippie, *Custer's Last Stand*, p. 50).

9. Otto Becker's, *Custer's Last Fight* (Dippie, *Custer's Last Stand*, pp. 53-54).

10. Thomas Hart Benton (Dippie, *Custer's Last Stand*, p. 54).

11. Custer as a child and Custer's body dead on the battlefield. (Russell, *Custer's Last*, p. 33).

12. H. K. Heinz Company (Dippie, *Custer's Last Stand*, p. 56).

13. Blanche Boies (Taft, Robert, A., "The Pictorial Record of the Old West: Custer's Last Stand - John Mulvaney, Cassilly Adams, and Otto Becker," in Paul Hutton's *The Custer Reader*, p. 444).

14. Edgar S. Paxson's *Custer's Last Stand* (Taft, from *Custer Reader*, p. 447).

15. Elk Eber's *Custer Last Battle* (Taft, from *Custer Reader*, p. 448).

16. Amon Carter Museum in Fort Worth, Texas (Russell, *Custer's Last*).

17. *Esquire and Colliers* (Dippie, *Custer's Last Stand*, p. 48).

18. John Mulvaney's *Custer's Last Rally* (Russell, *Custer's Last*, p. 28).

19. In excess of $50,000 (Dippie, *Custer's Last Stand,* p. 50).

20. American Oil Company (Russell, *Custer's Last,* p. 56).

21. Lucky Strikes (Dippie, *Custer's Last Stand.* p. 56.).

22. *Playboy* (Brown, Buck, *Playboy,* XIV (December, 1967), p. 193).

23. Foedor Fuchs (Dippie, *Custer's Last Stand,* p. 35).

24. Nick Eggenhoffer (Leighton, Margaret, *The Story of General Custer*).

25. Theodore Pittman (Dippie, *Custer's Last Stand,* p. 44).

26. Ernest L. Blumenschein (Dippie, *Custer's Last Stand,* p. 36).

27. *Following the Guidon* (Russell, *Custer's Last,* p. 44).

28. Richard Lorenz (Russell, *Custer's Last,* p. 39).

29. 12 x 32 feet (Dippie, *Custer's Last Stand,* p. 51).

30. Dr. Charles E. McChesney (Russell, *Custer's Last,* p. 25).

31. 11 x 32 feet (Dippie, *Custer's Last Stand,* p. 49).

32. William de la Montagne Cary (Russell, *Custer's Last,* p. 15).

33. Stanley Legowick (Russell, *Custer's Last,* p. 51).

34. James Kenneth Ralston (Dippie, *Custer's Last Stand,* p. 46).

35. Carl Lindeberg's *Beginning of the Charge That Wiped Out Custer and Das Ende.* (Russell, *Custer's Last,* p. 54).

36. Frederic Remington (Dippie, *Custer's Last Stand,* p. 37).

37. Frederic Remington (Dippie, *Custer's Last Stand,* p. 40).

38. Joe Grandee (Dippie, *Custer's Last Stand,* p. 46).

39. Leonard Baskin (Dippie, *Custer's Last Stand,* p. 47).

40. "Tumbleweeds" (Dippie, *Custer's Last Stand,* p. 60).

41. Custer's naked corpse by Leonard Baskin (Dippie, *Custer's Last Stand,* p. 47).

42. William Herbert Dunton's *The Custer Fight* (Taft, from *Custer Reader,* p. 448).

43. Newell Convers Wyeth (Dippie, *Custer's Last Stand,* p. 214).

44. Kurz and Allison (Russell, Don, *Custer's Last,* p. 22).

45. *The Battle of The Little Big Horn* by John Adams Elder (1884) (Russell, *Custer's Last,* pp. 49-50).

46. Nicholas Eggenhoffer (Dippie, *Custer's Last Stand,* p. 45).

47. Harold von Schmidt (Russell, *Custer's Last,* p. 45).

48. Eric von Schmidt (Hutton, *Custer Reader*, p. 89).

49. *Ellis's History of The United States* (Russell, *Custer's Last*, p. 62).

50. Elk Eber's *General Custer's Last Battle* (*Souvenir Program, 75th Anniversary of the Battle of the Little Big Horn*, 1951).

ANSWERS TO TRIVIA IN MOVIES & TV

1. Philip Carey (Hutton, Paul A., "Correct in Every Detail: General Custer in Hollywood," in Charles Rankin, editor, *Legacy: New Perspectives on the Battle of the Little Big Horn*, p. 254).

2. Capt. Myles Keogh (Hutton, from *Legacy*, p. 253).

3. Wayne Maunder (Hutton, from *Legacy*, p. 257).

4. John Litel (Thomas, Tony; Behlmer, Rudy; & McCarty, Clifford, *The Films of Errol Flynn*, p. 106).

5. Kieron Moore (*Custer of the West* Program Book, p. 10).

6. Filmed at the actual battlefield (Dippie, Brian W. *Custer's Last Stand: The Anatomy of an American Myth*, p. 115).

7. Richard Mulligan in *Little Big Man* and *Teachers* (Hutton, from *Legacy*, p. 270).

8. Western gunfighters (Hutton, from *Legacy*, p. 243).

9. Anthony Quinn (Hutton, from *Legacy*, p. 241).

10. Depicted Custer as graduating from West Point with Jeb Stuart in 1854 when Custer actually graduated in 1861 (Thomas; Behlmer; & McCarty, *Films of Errol Flynn*, p. 99).

11. Ronald Reagan (Hutton, from *Legacy*, p. 242).

12. Lieutenant. W. W. Cooke (Hutton, from *Legacy*, p. 245).

13. *The Dice of God* by Hoffman Birney (Hutton, from *Legacy*, p. 254).

14. *Broken Lance* (Dippie, *Custer's Last Stand*, p. 108).

15. Hugh Beaumont of *Leave It To Beaver* (from video of film, Republic, 1951).

16. Sidney Salkow (Dippie, *Custer's Last Stand*, p. 113).

17. Blythe Danner (from video of program, Warner Brothers, 1977).

18. Whit Bissell and Barry Atwater (Buscombe, Edward, editor, *The BFI Companion to the Western*, p. 107).

19. He disguised himself as an Indian (from video of program, Warner Brothers, 1960).

20. *She Wore a Yellow Ribbon.* (Dippie, *Custer's Last Stand,* p. 107).

21. Sidney Greenstreet (Thomas; Behlmer; & McCarty, *Films of Errol Flynn,* p. 106).

22. All played Crazy Horse in various films: Chief Thundercloud in *Buffalo Bill* (1944); Victor Mature in *Chief Crazy Horse* (1955); Will Sampson in *The White Buffalo* (1977); and Michael Greyeyes in *Crazy Horse* (1996), (Buscombe, BFT Companion, p. 107; and from video of program, Turner, 1996).

23. Peter Horton (from video of program, Turner, 1996).

24. *The Cowboys* (from video of program, Sanford Productions - Warner Brothers, 1971).

25. William Ludlow (from video of film).

26. *A Horse for Mrs. Custer* by Glendon Swarthout (Hutton, from *Legacy,* p. 253).

27. Both played California Joe (Thomas; Behlmer; & McCarty, *Films of Errol Flynn,* p. 106).

28. William Connors, Michael McCluskey, Richard Langsford (from video of program, CBS, 1958).

29. *F-Troop* (from video of program, Warner Brothers, 1965).

30. Jason McCord as played by Chuck Connors (from video of program, Reel World , 1991).

31. *The Seventh is Made Up of Phantoms* (from video of program, CBS, 1958).

32. Michael Curtis (Thomas; Behlmer; & McCarty, *Films of Errol Flynn,* p. 110.).

33. Raoul Walsh (Thomas; Behlmer; & McCarty, *Films of Errol Flynn,* p. 106; Hutton, from *Legacy,* p. 26).

34. *Son of the Morning Star* (Hutton from *Legacy,* p. 263).

35. Both screenplays written by Melissa Mathison (Hutton from *Legacy,* p. 263).

36. Gary Cole (Hutton from *Legacy,* p. 263).

37. *Touche pas la femme blanche* (Hutton, from *Legacy,* p. 261).

38. Douglas MacArthur (Hutton, from *Legacy,* p. 270).

39. Sheb Wooley (Eyles, *The Western,* p. 49).

40. "Goofs and Saddles" (from video of program, Columbia, 1937 / 1996).

41. *Custer's Last Fight* (1912) (Hutton, from *Legacy*, p. 252).

42. *The Scarlet West (1925); With General Custer at Little Big Horn* (1926); and *The Flaming Frontier* (1926) (Dippie, *Custer's Last Stand*, pp. 100-102).

43. Lloyd Bridges and John Ireland (Adams, Les, & Rainey, Buck, *Shoot-Em-Ups: The Complete Reference Guide to Westerns of the Sound Era*, p. 403).

44. David Appel's *Comanche* (Hutton, from *Legacy*, p. 253).

45. *Custer of the West* (Hutton, from *Legacy*, p. 259).

46. Kevin Costner (Hutton, from *Legacy*, p. 263).

47. Robert Lansing (Yoggy, Gary A., *Riding the Video Range: The Rise and Fall of the Western on Television*. p. 224).

48. Frank Kaquitts (Buscombe, *BFI Companion*, p. 221).

49. Rosanna Arquette (Hutton, from *Legacy*, p. 263).

50. Lasky Mesa (Thomas; Behlmer; & McCarty, *Films of Errol Flynn*, p. 109).

51. Clay Clement (Hutton, from *Legacy*, p. 236).

52. Chief Wolf Head (from video of program, Desilu, 1958).

53. Lenore Coffee (Hutton, from *Legacy*, p. 243).

54. *The Massacre* (1912) (Hutton, from *Legacy*, p. 236).

55. Bob Langdon (Hutton, from *Legacy*, p. 237).

56. *They Died With Their Boots On* (Hutton, from *Legacy:* p. 244).

57. Fort Apache (Hutton, from *Legacy*, p. 231).

58. Peter Ortiz (Hutton, from *Legacy*, p. 252).

59. Three died (Hutton, from *Legacy*, p. 244).

60. Joseph Cotten (Hutton, from *Legacy*, p. 254).

61. Alfred Waud (Hutton, from *Legacy*, p. 241).

62. *The Day Custer Fell* (Hutton, from *Legacy*, p. 255).

63. *Red Tomahawk* (Hutton, from *Legacy*, p. 255).

64. They all had episodes dealing with Custer (Dippie, *Custer's Last Stand*, pp. 118-119).

65. Rudy Montague played by Ron Leibman (Hutton, from *Legacy*, p. 270).

66. *The Legend of the Lone Ranger* (Hutton, from *Legacy,* p. 270).

67. She was the real-life wife of actor Robert Shaw who played Custer (Program Book of *Custer of the West*, p. 8).

68. Britt Lomand (Hutton, from *Legacy,* p. 253).

69. Walter Brennan (Hutton, from *Legacy,* p. 243).

70. $1,357.00 (Hutton, from *Legacy,* p. 243).

71. *Buffalo Bill's Indian Wars* (Hutton, from *Legacy,* p. 235).

72. *The Flaming Frontier* (Hutton, from *Legacy*, p. 237).

73. *The Flaming Frontier* (Dippie, *Custer's Last Stand*, p. 101).

74. Ned Finley (Hutton, from *Legacy,* p. 236).

75. Frank McGlynn (Hutton, from *Legacy*, p. 241).

76. Iron Eyes Cody (Buscombe, *BFT Companion,* p. 332).

77. General McCabe (Hutton, from *Legacy,* p. 254).

78. Leslie Nielsen (Eyles, *The Western*, p. 135).

79. James Olsen (Hutton, from *Legacy*, p. 258).

80. J. Carroll Naish in *Annie Get Your Gun* (MGM, 1950) and *Sitting Bull* (United Artists, 1954), (Eyles, *The Western*, p. 135).

81. Crazy Horse (Yoggy, *Riding the Video*, p. 389).

82. Arikara, Cheyenne, Crow, Sioux (from production notes of film).

83. Floyd Red Crow Westerman (Yoggy, *Riding the Video*, p. 389).

84. *"Gold, Glory and Custer - Prelude* and *Gold, Glory and Custer - Requiem* (Yoggy, *Riding the Video*, p. 192).

85. Lorne Greene (Yoggy, *Riding the Video*, p. 192).

86. A watch that plays *Garry Owen* (from video of program, Reel World, 1991).

87. Grant Williams (from video of program, Official Films, 1959).

88. *Wyoming* (Hutton, *Custer Reader*, p. 498)

89. Douglass Kennedy (Hutton, *Custer Reader*, p. 508)

90. Ty Hardin played Reno and Jeffrey Hunter played Benteen (Hutton, from *Legacy,* p. 259; *Custer of the West* Program Book, p. 7).

91. Joshua Lucas (from video of program, Universal, 1992).

92. Sheldon Wolfchild (Yoggy, *Riding the Video*, p. 389).

93. Roy Bancroft (Hutton, from *Legacy,* p. 241).

94. Captain Benteen (from video of program, Desilu, 1957).

95. *Son of The Morning Star* (from video of program, Republic, 1991).

96. Ed Lauter (from video of film, United Artists, 1977).

97. James Millican (Hutton, from *Legacy,* p. 251).

98. *Dr. Quinn Medicine Woman* (from video of program, CBS, 1993, 1996).

99. James Millican (Hutton, from *Custer Reader,* p. 497).

100. *Custer's Last Fight* (1912) (Dippie, *Custer's Last Stand*, p. 89).

Movie poster from 1936 movie and 15 part serial from Vincent A. Heier Collection.

Front and back cover of flyer promoting the 1936 movie and 15 part serial from Vincent A. Heier Collection..

*Interior advertising copy from flyer promoting the 1936 movie and
15 part serial from Vincent A. Heier Collection..*

BIBLIOGRAPHY

Adams, Les, & Rainey, Buck, *Shoot-Em-Ups: The Complete Reference Guide to Westerns of the Sounds* Era, Waynesville, NC: World of Yesterday.

Alter, Judy, *Libbie: A Novel of Elizabeth Bacon Custer*, New York: Bantam, 1994.

Appel, Allen, *Twice Upon a Time*, New York: Carroll & Graf Publishers, 1988.

Amaral, Anthony A., *Comanche: The Horse That .Survived the Custer Massacre,* Los Angeles :Westernlore Press, 1961.

Barton, Del, *A Good Day to Die*, Garden City, NY: Doubleday, 1980.

Berger, Thomas, *Little Big Man,* New York: Dial Press, 1964.

Birney, Hoffman, *The Dice of God,* New York: Henry Holt, 1956.

Blackburn, Thomas Wakefield, *A Good Day to Die*, New York: Popular Library, 1967.

Blake, Michael, *Marching to Valhalla,* New York: Villard, 1996.

Blevins, Will, *Stone Song*, New York: Tom Doherty, 1995.

Brady, Cyrus T., *Britton of the Seventh: A Romance of Custer and the Great Northwest*, Chicago: A.C. McClurg, 1914.

Brautigan, Richard, *The Pill Versus the Springhill Mine Disaster,* New York: Dell Publishing Co., 1973.

Brown, R. D., Kranidas, Thomas & Norris, Faith G., editors, *Oregon Signatures,* Mommouth, OR: Oregon State College, 1959.

Burdick, Usher, *Tragedy in the Great Sioux Camp* Baltimore: Proof Press, 1936.

Ceremonies Attending the Unveiling of the Equestrian Statue to Major General George Armstrong Custer by the State of Michigan and Formally Dedicated at the City of Monroe, Michigan, June Fourth, Nineteen Hundred Ten, n.p.n.d. (1910).

Chief, Eagle, D., *Winter Count,* Denver: Golden Bell Press, 1968.

Chivantone, Frederick J., *A Road We Do Not Know: A Novel of Custer at the Little Bighorn*, New York: Simon & Schuster, 1996.

Clark, Kathy, *Cody's Last Stand*, Toronto: Harlequin, 1992.

Crawford, Jack, *The Poet Scout: A Book of Song* and Story , New York: Funk & Wagnells, 1886,

Dippie, Brian W., *Custer's Last Stand: The Anatomy of an American Myth,* Lincoln: University of Nebraska Press, 1976, 1994.

Dippie, Brian & Carroll, John, *Bards of the Little Big Horn*, Bryan, TX: Guidon Press.

Custer of the West Program Book, England: Upton Printing Group.

Drago, Harry Sinclair, *Montana Road*, New York: William Morrow, 1935.

Dugan, Bill, *Crazy Horse: War Chiefs,* New York: Harper, 1992.

Fairman, Paula, *The Tender and the Savage,* Los Angeles, Pinnacle, 1980.

Fraser, George MacDonald, *Flashman and the Redskins* New York: Alfred A. Knopf, 1982.

Fisher, Clay, *Yellow Hair,* Boston: Houghton Mifflin, 1957.

Foreman, L. L., *The Renegade,* New York: Belmont, 1971.

Fraser, George MacDonald, *Flashman and the Redskins,* New York: Alfred A. Knopf, 1982.

Garland, Hamlin, "The Silent Eaters," in *The Book of the American Indian,* New York: Harper & Brothers, 1923.

Goshe, Frederick & Goshe, Frank, *The Dauntless and the Dreamers,* New York: Thomas Yoseloff, 1963.

Gould, Theodore Anthony, Teat, *The Saga of an American Frontiersman,* Bellingham, WA: World Promotions, 1986.

Graham, W. A., *The Custer Myth* Harrisburg, PA: Stackpole, 1953.

Green, Charles P., *Ballads of the Black Hills,* Boston: The Christopher Publishing House, 1931.

Gruber, Frank, *Bugles West,* New York: Rinehart, 1954.

Haycox, Ernest, *Bugles in the Afternoon,* Boston: Little, Brown, 1944.

Henry, Will, *No Survivors,* New York: Random House, 1950.

Hutton, Paul A., "Correct in Every Detail: General Custer in Hollywood," in Charles Rankin, editor, *Legacy: New Perspectives on the Battle of the Little Bighorn,* Helena, MT: Montana Historical Society Press, 1996.

Hutton, Paul A., editor, *The Custer Reader,* Lincoln: University of Nebraska Press, 1992.

Johnston, Terry C., *Long Winter Gone,* New York: Bantam, 1990.

Johnston, Terry C., *Seize the Sky,* New York: Bantam, 1991.

Johnston, Terry C., *Whisper of the Wolf,* New York: Bantam, 1991.

Johnstone, William W., *The Scream of Eagles,* New York: Pinnacle Books, 1996.

Jones, Douglas C., *The Court-Martial of George Armstrong Custer,* New York: Charles Scribner's, 1976.

LeCaine, John, (Woonkapi-Sni), "Custer's Day," in *The Sioux Indians in Canada* by Gontran LaViolette, Regina, Sask.: The Marian Press, 1944.

Leighton, Margaret, *The Story of General Custer,* New York: Grossett & Dunlap, 1954.

Longfellow, Henry W., *The Youth's Companion,* (March 1, 1877).

MacKaye, Loring, *The Great Scoop,* New York: Thomas Nelson, 1956.

McClurg, A. C. *Molly McDonald: A Tale of the Old Frontier,* Chicago: A. C. McClurg, 1912.

Mills, Charles, *A Mighty Afternoon,* Garden City, NY: Doubleday, 1980.

Monaghan, Jay, *Custer: The Life of General George Armstrong Custer,* Boston: Little Brown & Co.

Morford, Henry, "Chivalry's Afterglow" in *Algernon Sydney Sullivan,* by Anne Middleton Holmes, New York Southern Society, 1929.

Murray, Earl, *Thunder in the Dawn,* New York: Tom Doherty, 1993.

Myrick, Herbert, *Cache la Poudre: The Romance of a Tenderfoot in the Days of Custer,* New York: Orange Judd, 1905.

Neihardt, John G., *The Song of the Indian Wars*, New York: The Macmillan Co., 1925.

Nichols, Ronald H., *In Custer's Shadow: Marcus Reno*, Fort Collins: Old Army Press, 1999.

Norris, P. W., *The Calumet of the Couteau and Other Poetical Legends of the Border*, Philadelphia: J. B. Lippincott, 1883.

Oliver, Chad, *Broken Eagle*, New York: Bantam, 1989.

Parrish, Randall, *Bob Hampton of Placer,* Chicago, 1906.

Patten, Lewis B., *The Red Sabbath,* Garden City, NY: Doubleday, 1968

Ralston, J. K., *The Custer Mystery*, Crow Agency, MT: Custer Battlefield National Monument, ca. 1960.

Rankin, Charles E., *Legacy, New Perspectives on the Battle of the Little Bighorn*, Helena, MT: Montana Historical Society, 1996.

Russell, Don, *Custer's Last* Ft. Worth, TX: Amon Carter Museum, 1968.

Safire, William, *Freedom,* Garden City, NY: Doubleday, 1987.

Sandoz, Mari, *Crazy Horse: Strange Man of the Oglalla*, New York: Hastings House, 1975.

Shiflet, Kenneth E., *The Convenient Coward,* Harrisburg, PA: Stackpole, 1961.

Simmerlee, Maud M., *United States History in Rhyme*, New York: Herman Lechner, 1911.

Smith, Martin Cruz, *The Indians Won*, New York: Belmont, 1970.

Souvenir Program, 75th Anniversary of the Battle of the Little Big Horn, Billings, MT, 1951.

Taft, Robert, "The Pictorial Record of the Old West: Custer's Last Stand-- John Mulvaney, Cassily Adams, and Otto Becker," in Paul Hutton's *The Custer Reader*, 1992.

Teepee Book, The, II (June, 1916).

Thomas, Tony; Behlmer, Rudy; & McCarty, Clifford, *The Films of Errol Flynn*, New York: Citadel Press, 1969.

Travers, Col. J. M., *Custer's Last Shot; or The Boy Trailer of the Little Big Horn*, Wide Awake Library, No. 565, 1883.

Utley, Steven & Waldrop, Howard, "Custer's Last Jump," in Terri Carr's *The Best Science Fiction of the Year #6*, New York: Ballantine, 1977.

Vaughan, Robert, *Yesterday's Reveille,* New York: St. Martin's, 1996.

Waight, Quentin, *Prelude to Glory*, Seattle: Superior Publishing, 1951.

Walker, Judson Elliot, *Campaigns of General Custer in the North-West, and the Final Surrender of Sitting Bull*, New York: 1881.

Webb, Laura S., *Custer's Immortality: A Poem With Biographical Sketches of the Chief Actors in the Late Tragedy of the Wilderness*, New York: New York Evening Post Steam Presses, 1876.

Wilcox, Ella Wheeler, *Custer, and Other Poems*, Chicago: W.B. Conkley Co., 1896.

Wister, G. Clifton, *Lakota,* New York: Zebra Books, 1989.

Yoggy, Gary A., *Riding the Video Range: The Rise and Fall of the Western on Television.* Jefferson, NC: McFarland, 1995.

Ceremonies Attending the Unveiling of the Equestrian Statue to Major General George Armstrong Custer by the State of Michigan, and Formally Dedicated at the City of Monroe. Michigan, June Fourth, Nineteen Hundred Ten, n.p. n.d. (1910) pp. 119-120; cf. Dippie & Carroll, *Bards*.

The Teepee Book, II (June, 1916), p. 13; cf. Dippie & Carroll, *Bards*, p. 224.

Program Book of *Custer of the West*, England: Upton Printing Group, p.10

Souvenir Program. 75th Anniversary of the Battle of the Little Big Horn, Billings, MT, 1951.